POETOPIA

THE WEST MIDLANDS

Edited by Lisa Adlam

First published in Great Britain in 2015 by:

Young**Writers**

Remus House
Coltsfoot Drive
Peterborough
PE2 9BF
Telephone: 01733 890066
Website: www.youngwriters.co.uk

All Rights Reserved
Book Design by **ASHLEY JANSON**
© Copyright Contributors 2015
SB ISBN 978-1-78443-608-7

Printed and bound in the UK by BookPrintingUK
Website: www.bookprintinguk.com

FOREWORD

Welcome, Reader!

For Young Writers' latest competition, Poetopia, we gave secondary school pupils nationwide the challenge of writing a poem based on the rules of one of 5 factions: Castitas for reflective, honest poetry; Temperantia for angry, assertive poetry; Humilitas for positive, uplifting poetry; Benevolentia for emotional poetry; and Industria for diligent, structured poetry. Poets who wrote a poem outside of these parameters were assigned to Dissimĭlis.

We chose poems for publication based on style, expression, imagination and technical skill. The result is this entertaining collection full of diverse and imaginative poetry, which is also a delightful keepsake to look back on in years to come.

Here at Young Writers our aim is to encourage creativity in the next generation and to inspire a love of the written word, so it's great to get such an amazing response, with some absolutely fantastic poems. Once all the books in the series are published we will pick the best poem from each faction to win a prize.

I'd like to congratulate all the young poets in **Poetopia - The West Midlands** - I hope this inspires them to continue with their creative writing. And who knows, maybe we'll be seeing their names on the best seller lists in the future...

Jenni Bannister
Editorial Manager

THE FACTIONS

CASTITAS (Kas-ti-tas)

- Write a soul-baring, honest poem
- Tell us what it is like to be you
- Channel your confusion and emotions at being a teenager into verse

TEMPERANTIA (Temper-ran-tee-ah)

- Stand up for someone or something
- Vent your anger through poetry
- Express your frustration about a situation that's out of your control

HUMILITAS (Hu-mil-lih-tahs)

- Write a positive, uplifting poem
- Write an ode to celebrate someone or something that you appreciate
- Write a spiritual poem

BENEVOLENTIA (Ben-e-vol-en-tee-ah)

- Write a love / emotional poem
- Empathise with another's situation or predicament
- Write a praise poem
- Write a poem about your best friend / your friendship

INDUSTRIA (In-dust-ree-ah)

- Write a poem about current affairs
- Use a strict poetic form, such as a sonnet or kyrielle
- Research a poet of your choice and write in a similar style

DISSIMĬLIS (Diss-i-mĭl-is)

- If pupils write a poem that falls outside of the factions' rules, they become Dissimĭlis
- Poems can be on any theme or style

CONTENTS

THE
POEMS

Emile Heskey

Emile Heskey
England's number nine
Used to play for villa
Can't run down the line

He always misses
Goal in his sight
Surprisingly
It goes over head height

As the goal kick comes back
The ball is won
It is passed to Heskey
Can he actually score this one?

Emile Heskey
He is so bad
He plays for Bolton
And he is very sad.

Harry Tudge (13)

Enemy Be Gone

Running and sprinting from the wicked enemy
Finding and searching for his destiny
Been hit by
Trying not to cry
Being reported
Been unsupported
Glimpse upon glimpse of blood
Been stabbed with a sharp piece of wood
Running and sprinting from the wicked enemy
Now found his destiny
A friend!

Schinda Blackwood (11)

Our Depressed Darkness

I wish I could stop
This blackness within
I wish I could love you right
But I cannot

I wish I could show you
But you'd never listen
It makes this hole within bigger
But you cannot see, my precious blinded

I love you so
A poisoned death
Fixed in time
I just wish it not

All others standing around
Pushing, shoving, laughing, joking
I want it to stop
For there to be eternal peace

But even in silence still
I cannot find the promised peace
This piercing scream
Where from?

Blinded anger
Coursing through my veins
Forgive me, my love
The darkness is alive

I tried to stop
But you only made it worse
These people around
Chaos, destruction, burning, breaking

Stop!
But it continues to flow
Stop!
But it continues to grow

Scarlet blood flowing around
The dagger from our lips
So much like the pretty little rose
I compared to you

At the beginning
All was well
But it was not all it seemed
For all was locked away

I tried, I promise I did
But all you will ever see
Is my failure
And the crushing sadness and grief

No cure to this pain
In my mind, soul, heart
Remains, it will not go
Taking my faith

All is gone
All but you
All but you, my darkness.

Sidrah Farooq (16)
Abu Bakr Primary School, Walsall

A First World War Poem

War is like hell on Earth
A time when the sun doesn't shine
Bloodshed, brutality and gruesome death
The pain is a frozen knife, stabbing you!

So cold even snowflakes would shiver
The trenches are pits of nightmare and misery
Where soldiers ponder if they'll be a survivor
All you see in their eyes is fear and worry

The constant sound of gunfire is death calling you
Every sound you hear is suddenly relentless
The water you walk in is filthy and bloody
You have no choice but to march through it defenceless

You are trapped inside a horror movie
Where your only escape is death!

Zareen Fatema
Abu Bakr Primary School, Walsall

Defeat

Blood starts to drip from the soldier's wounds
Seeps like sewage beneath the soil

Deep in the house, white is fading to red
And the freedom we're fighting for seems to be dead
Because we can't win like he once said
No we can't triumph over the hate
But we're deep in mud over the disgusting food we've been fed

The wind is blowing like a hurricane over our heads
In the frightening, desolated lands
Where wolves are going insane
And hawks are feasting on dead soldiers

Bullets are flying, children are dying
Mothers are crying
While the enemies are hiding
Behind the walls that no one is looking at
God knows the truth

Too many hands are wiping away widowers' tears
Gunshots are ringing in people's ears
Too many frozen hearts frozen from their own fears
Hopes too distant, like sky chandeliers

Consistent nightmares of escaping
We grasp our weapons with hope in our hearts
My dry lips whisper a final prayer to God hoping for the best
Before a gunshot is echoed
Through the air, someone falls

Looking at the cloudless horizon
Ashes are everywhere
What a war!
There are so many bodies lying around
But the dead are hoping
That we will win the next war.

Sarah Salmah (12)
Abu Bakr Primary School, Walsall

The River's Race

S tarting at a gentle flow
T he river doesn't mind being slow
R elaxed and steady on its path
E asy going, not too fast
A iming for the ocean wide
M eandering here, soon joining the tide

R oaring along at a tremendous pace
A s if competing in a race
P rancing, dancing, galloping along
I t pushes its way through leafy, green fronds
D iamond-like rocks litter the way
S crambling over them, rushing away

W andering past jagged rocks and streams
A nd laughing and gurgling in the sunbeams
T rying to reach the cliff's sharp edge
E njoying the thought of tumbling over the ledge
R oaring and shouting, it gains its pace
F rantically trying to win the race
A gainst all the other rivers and streams
L ashing and crashing, while they all twinkle and gleam
L unging forward, over the edge it goes
S plashing noisily, scaring off nearby crows

O nce again on its path
C rashings and tumblings are long since past
E nding its life's journey at the beach
A nd trying to see how far up it can reach
N ever to compete again, its goal reached at last.

Aasiyah Mirza (12)
Abu Bakr Primary School, Walsall

My Love

My love has a name which reflects her,
Nothing can be more dear.
My love is very modest,
She is probably the greatest.
My love is very royal,
And she is also very loyal.
My love belongs to me.

My love cuddles with me,
Her body curls around me beautifully.
My love has a colourful coat,
Much better than a silly old boat.
My love will always be at my side,
So I want to spread her name worldwide.
My love belongs to me.

My love has emerald eyes,
Which I stare at with pride.
My love never gets old for fun and games,
Her ideas are like a maze.
My love has the most cutest face ever,
Nothing else can look better.
My love belongs to me.

My love makes the most adorable noises ever,
They cannot be written on paper.
My love has magnificent whiskers,
Much better than flowers.
My love has delicate paws,
But hidden inside are sharp claws.
My love is my calico cat, Twinkle.

Madiha Akther Esha (12)
Abu Bakr Primary School, Walsall

She's Mine

She's my friend,
My companion,
When I'm down,
I know where to turn,
She's my safe,
With locks and chains,
The one I confide,
My tear and pains.

She's my angel in disguise,
Cheers me up when a part of me dies,
She holds my hand and says she'll be there,
That's when I know she really cares.

She understands my fears,
Stands there wiping her tears,
When I need something to hide,
She's always by my side.

Friendship is a beautiful thing,
You need it when something is happening,
To be there to console you,
To understand too.

Through all the hardship days,
It's like chasing you through a maze,
That's the best thing about it,
You'll always have the friends that are there,
Till the very end.

Sayma Siddikha
Abu Bakr Primary School, Walsall

Shadows

Mysteriously following you like a stalker,
Hiding in the dark as if it's afraid,
Standing by you like a walker,
You wonder why it was made?

It feels like a dark presence behind you,
It's an exact copy of your own self,
You know wherever you go, it'll be there too,
You realise everyone else has one, not just yourself.

As the day goes on, the taller it gets,
Watching you like a hawk,
But as the sun sets,
It's like it's gone for a long walk.

In the evening, it's not there,
No matter where you look,
It's gone and you wonder where?
It's like it's just been took.

When the sun appears, it comes back,
Copying your every move like your own reflection,
Like it's ready to attack,
All you can do is stare at your complexion.

Then the rain starts to fall,
It leaves my sight off to the meadow,
Finally leaving the floor and the wall,
Realising it was your shadow . . .

Hafsa Aisha Akhtar (11)
Abu Bakr Primary School, Walsall

When Hope Dies

The cooling breeze, blows all my leaves
Down onto the ground
And all the trees, with all the leaves
Murmur amongst themselves

I used to have the squirrel and birds
Who'd constantly surround me
Even the trees who were my friends
Now cannot stand me

In the chilly winter, they huddle together
Leaving me aside
Why, oh why, am I left alone
Am I a pesticide?

And I'm left there, standing bare
Away from all the trees
Why is the feeling of despair
Growing inside of me?

Walking now, to the abyss
I leave the world that I now miss
Accompanied by my only friend
A small majestic robin
The one who came when I was down
The one who kept me safe and sound
The one who came and who stayed
With the forgotten tree, in the shade.

Tahseen Zaynab Yusuf
Abu Bakr Primary School, Walsall

Social Media

How we love social media
But sometimes you have to be safe
Twitter, Facebook and Instagram
All to keep updated with your fam
Talk to new people
Share your life with people
Meet different people
But then you find they're not interested in you

Be harsh, be nasty, be rude
This will all upset your happy mood
Don't have a fight even though they start it
It might lead to something major
It might even put you in danger

This adds up to you breaking up
You're in a dream
No real friends in that world
Now you're sitting in the corner, curled
Frightened, scared, not knowing what to do
Well I know
Get into the real world
Yes, reality
Real life, real people, real you!

Sabah Akhtar (12)
Abu Bakr Primary School, Walsall

In The Clouds

In the clouds is where my head lies when I go to say my beddy byes
I twirl with my teddy ever so high that I always land at the top of the sky
I stand at the top of the sky
I won't look down or frown with all my might I try to keep my eyes open
Eventually they do and drift back into bed . . .

Hannah Hasinah Hussain (11)
Abu Bakr Primary School, Walsall

Poverty Cannot Be Ignored!

Poverty, such an unhelpful thing
People bearing such little things
Food, heating and drink
They just want to live a blissful life

Not a life to tear apart
But to stay in a home like every other
Tears are powerful which cannot be ignored
Tears are a sign which shows they need you

Flowers blooming day and night
That's how they want to live a normal life
Their estate is a dangerous place
Thunder and lightning will keep them fighting

Children, vulnerable, isolated
When the night sky falls they call
No one to stand by their side
Hardships, difficultly is all they have to bear

You now know that they really care
Now you understand you can give them a hand
At the end of the day darkness brings light, we all are a creation
It's always good to do a positive action, not a negative action.

Habibah Kamran (12)
Abu Bakr Primary School, Walsall

Innocence

As the morning rises, you rouse from your sleep
Jumping out of bed with a smile on your face
Your heart is in grace as soon as your eyes set
The bright light shining on your face
The ball of happiness
The golden ray, a piece of treasure
There you are, my sun!

Aamina Ramzan (11)
Abu Bakr Primary School, Walsall

Why She's Great . . .

When I had fallen she helped me stand.
She would put everything right, when I had nothing planned.
When I cried, she gently wiped my tears away.
For success in my life, she'll always pray.

When I was sick, she was always by my side.
In every stage of life I need her as my guide.
When others had hurt me and said unkind words at school.
She taught me how to stand up to myself, so I don't look like a fool.

When I was all lonely and had nothing to do.
She came to make me laugh, it's true.
When I got all stressed and went all mad.
She would help me, for that I am glad.

When I was scared, up in my bed.
She would surely come, I knew it in my head.
When I was hungry, she gave me food.
For that I was always in a happy mood.

Oh Mum, how can I thank you for all you have done?
In my life you are the bright sun.
Oh Mum, how can I thank you for all you have done?
You taught me how to face my fears, before I run.

Saarah Saeedah (12)
Abu Bakr Primary School, Walsall

My Brother

Even though you are not with me I will still love you with my heart
You left this world and brought a tear to my eye
No matter what happens I'll stay by your side and never let you go
You are my brother and I am your sister
I'll love you forever and won't forget you.

Suhaylah Bryan (11)
Abu Bakr Primary School, Walsall

Fear

Waking up the next day
You decided you wanted to stay
The fear kicked in
And you ran straight towards the bin

Fearing something would happen your face turned white
And you scrunched it up tight
You were more awake than ever before
And you kept glancing towards the door

You were so scared
As if you knew this would happen
It's like you were dared
So you stayed quiet in case you were heard

Running to the bathroom
You threw up all your food
Onto the floor it went
And left behind the horrible scent

Why are you so scared?
Why be quiet so you're not heard?
Why glance towards the door?
Like you never have before.

Aisha Hussain (13)
Abu Bakr Primary School, Walsall

Temper, Temper

Breathe in, breathe out
Try not to frown
Don't let your temper make you down
This temper, temper is a clown

Keep it in, don't let it out
No matter what they say
Don't scream, don't shout
It's a matter of time before you let your anger flow

Temper, temper is just a name
It's not suitable for your age

Please, oh please don't be furious
This temper is making me curious
We'll make you happy, not sad
We'll control it, so you don't stay mad
We'll find a cure, we'll make sure

We'll help you, that's why we're here
To help you get rid of this
Temper, temper

Oh, this temper . . .

Imaan Mahmood (12)
Abu Bakr Primary School, Walsall

A Friend Is...

A friend is someone who makes you laugh
A friend is someone who makes you cry
A friend is someone who makes you feel at home
A friend is trustworthy, loyal and precious, that friend is you!
Friends do fight
But you have to realise the true colours of life
And that friend might just be your best mistake in life.

Maryam Bibi (14)
Abu Bakr Primary School, Walsall

My Best Friend

My best friend,
She's as sweet as sugar,
I don't know what I'd do without her.

She's kind,
She's gentle,
And she's perfect for me.

I love her,
She loves me,
We talk and laugh,
And have the best day ever.

I'll be gloomy, when she's not there,
I chat on the phone with her,
And be happy all over again.

My best friend,
Sweet as sugar,
I don't know what I'd do without her!

Malaika Humaira Amin (11)
Abu Bakr Primary School, Walsall

Her Dark Thoughts . . .

She was sunken deep, into her dark thoughts
The loneliness, the darkness was her only paradise
She was destined to cut, her blood ruby red so appealing
It was easier to begin, than to quit
She closed her eyes, finding relief in her blade
Her scars were real, but so was the pain
She was sorry for being such a disappointment
But this was her fate, she was worthless
Why couldn't she believe in them, why couldn't she fit in?
She knew for a fact she was close enough to disappear into this twilight . . .
And so she did!

Aaishah Perager (14)
Abu Bakr Primary School, Walsall

Reading, Reading

Reading, reading,
It's what I do best.
It leads me on
And I can't take a rest.

Lost in a world,
Of fiction and fantasy,
There's darkness,
Waiting to come after me.

Here comes the happy ending,
The prince gets the princess.
And the wicked witch lies,
As still as the night.

Reading, reading,
It's what I do best.
It leads me on
And I can't take a rest.

Ayesha Patel (12)
Abu Bakr Primary School, Walsall

Friendship For Ever . . .

Friends are always close to your side,
Held on to you tight,
Always stay together,
Or you will lose each other forever,
Be together as long as you can,
Otherwise friendship can take an end,
Friends are for life,
If you break up then later you will
Feel the pain like you were stabbed with a knife,
Have the best mate,
And you will have a good fate.

Sabiya Khatun
Abu Bakr Primary School, Walsall

Wonderful Seasons

December, January and February
Winter is temporary
The world has gone white
And the snow is cold and will bite

March, April and May
It's Mother's Day
New flowers grow
And there's daffodils below

August, July and June
It'll be really good to go outside in the afternoon
Playing and having fun
In the shining sun

November, October and September
We should be an autumn member
The cool breeze
And leaves falling off trees.

Aaisha Diler (12)
Abu Bakr Primary School, Walsall

War

War is something that never ends
My dad gets a letter telling him he has to go to war
He tells us the news and I get scared more and more
He packs his stuff ready to fight
I have faith and hold on tight
He steps out the door no longer to be seen
Who knows if he'll be back from where he has been?
Months go by and I wonder where he is
I get the news and my heart breaks into pieces
I think about all the stuff he gave me
Now I realise how painful it is to lose a loved one.

Aisha Ashraf (12)
Abu Bakr Primary School, Walsall

Demons

Demons are such humorous creatures,
Taking your breath away, senseless.
They taunt you, tease you,
Until you're mentally black and blue.

Demons are such humorous creatures,
Telling you jokes yet truths.
Giggling in ridicule,
At your every single action.

Demons are such witty creatures,
Constantly snickering beside your ear.
Their games are endless, everlasting,
Until you can't fight anymore.

Demons are such peculiar creatures,
Most wonder why they are there.
My theory is that they're harrowing tests,
Constantly making you weep in despair.

Farzana Ali
Abu Bakr Primary School, Walsall

Times Go By As Lies

As times go by,
Wasted by lies,
And you ask why,
Why do you lie,
But your lies I don't buy,
Wasting your time on lies,
Use your time wisely,
And you'll see why,
You spend your time telling lies,
Why, why, why?

Imania Lubna Faheeb (11)
Abu Bakr Primary School, Walsall

Hope

I wipe the tears off my eyes,
Not making you realise,
That behind all this a story lies,
Sour as a lemon or sweet as pies.

This pain is just unbearable,
My tears have now created a flood,
This is all unbelievable
I think next will be blood . . .

I wish and I pray
That this torture will go away,
I feel like I'm living in hell,
So shy I'm hiding underneath a shell.

I try to make every day the best it can be,
I hope you understand me,
I hope you see all the bad things that are happening to me,
I really hope you see.

Faheemah Lorgat
Abu Bakr Primary School, Walsall

My Life

Life is full of bad, difficulties and hatred
No one cares about what you are or who you are
It's like the whole world is against you
And that the dreaded is possible and fantasies are impossible
There's no one on Earth who understands you and your existence is
insignificant
You're always dropping to your knees and the flashbacks won't stop
Especially when it's still happening
You feel like there's nothing left of you now and if there is
Where has it gone?

Anisha Nadim
Abu Bakr Primary School, Walsall

Life's Harsh Race

I weep, I cry
No one knows my pain
The sorrow, the misery
Is that all I gain

When was the last time
I had a smile on my face
Why is life playing
Such a harsh race

Laughing and giggling
I hear from a corner
Never had I thought
I would be such a loner

Life has gone by
The pain is still there
I close my eyes
It all comes back again.

Nuha Aziz (12)
Abu Bakr Primary School, Walsall

Free Palestine, Free Gaza

Free, free Palestine
Free, free Gaza

Put your knives down
Put your guns down
Put your bombs down
And pray!

Why kill innocent people
Bin your knife and get a life.

Zaynab Siddiq (12)
Abu Bakr Primary School, Walsall

Emotions

Anger . . .
Is something that I cringe at in disgust
Sadness . . .
Is something that makes me feel like I'm nothing but dust
Fear . . .
Is something that haunts and gets me screaming
Jealousy . . .
Is something that I hate but can't help feeling
And joy . . .
The main emotion I feel every day
These emotions, they scare me, but help me in a way
They keep me secure, with all their might
Making my heart beam with light
Your emotions may hurt you, maybe even worse
Making you feel like your head is about to burst
But always remember and never forget
Your emotions are with you, something you'll never regret . . .

Amal Yusuf (11)
Abu Bakr Primary School, Walsall

Why Not Help?

Helping each other is what I do
Without this I don't know who I'd be
Everyone should be like me
Because this is what we should be

Problems, problems, this is it!
Come by me I'll solve it
As I said, I do this
Don't forget, I like this

We as people need to care a lot more about others
As people these days are really selfish
Again don't forget there's more like me!

Maniha Javed (12)
Abu Bakr Primary School, Walsall

My Anger

The anger inside me
Was too much to see
The thought that thousands of people are dying
Over two countries fighting
They are so into fighting
Do they even care for those who are dying?
It makes me wonder
If they ever ponder
Over killing the innocent and the needy
Do they ever feel guilty
For joining the army
Why can't they just come up with a plan
To resolve the problem of every man
Why take innocent lives?
Just make an effort to get along with other tribes
Apologising and sharing would cause no harm
It would only keep everyone cool and calm.

Sumaiya Nana
Abu Bakr Primary School, Walsall

I Am Temperantia

I feel angry and frustrated most of the time
Sometimes I even feel like committing a crime

Sometimes I wish people knew what it's like to be me
Why can't they ever see?

I need a helping hand
Someone who will understand

I always work hard
But I seem to fall harder

I seem to think I'm Industria
But really I'm Temperantia.

Kinza Khan (11)
Abu Bakr Primary School, Walsall

What A Friend Is . . .

Throughout my life you've been there for me
When I've had my ups and downs
You've always been the one to cheer me up
When I'm in a frown
You've been the sister I could never imagine
You're like a shooting star
Thank you for your kindness
You've given me so far.

You've earned a space in my heart
We're never far apart
I never said you're perfect
But you're definitely worth it
We've lived those memories together
I hope they last forever
There's not much more I can say
Apart from thank you for every single day.

Madeeha Arshad (12)
Abu Bakr Primary School, Walsall

My Mom

Mom, Mom, you're the best
You're not just my mom but my best friend
Without you who would feed, dress me
And be there for me?
And who will take my side on
Every step I take if
You weren't there?
Mom, you're just great

Every time I frown, you are there
To turn it upside-down
You've taught me to live and face my fears
Without you I wouldn't be who I am today.

Thahmina Ahmed (11)
Abu Bakr Primary School, Walsall

Be Ashamed To Bully!

Do not bully, it's so sad,
The victim will think, 'Am I really that bad?'
When you join a group and bully together,
It will stay with the victim forever and ever.
Once they go home, crying and upset,
You will start to feel bad and upset,
They don't come to school, they're too scared,
When the teacher finds out, you are dead.
They come to school to face their fears,
But fat, ugly and stupid is what you hear,
Then you realise your mistake,
And ask them to forgive you for all the hate.

Now let's stop bullying once and for all,
And let's fly together, let's not crawl.
All of this is done now and fully,
So just remember, be ashamed to bully!

Rahimah Begum (12)
Abu Bakr Primary School, Walsall

Racism

I'm black, I'm brown, I'm yellow and white
Seems to me this is in the light
People stare and give me looks
It's like a fish escaping a hook
Am I different from the rest?
They walk around thinking they're the best.

It shouldn't matter how I look
Or the colour of my skin
It shouldn't matter how I pray
Or what God I believe in
So it really shouldn't matter the colour of our birth
At the end of the day, we were all born on the same Earth.

Sadiyah Jahan (12)
Abu Bakr Primary School, Walsall

Your Mother

Your love is like a rose
Red and bright
The way you talk
The way you walk
Is all I like

The way you care
The way you share
Is all I like

The way you feed me
The way you dress me
Is what I like best

Always be thankful for your mother
No matter what
She's always there for you
No matter what happens.

Esha Fazal (11)
Abu Bakr Primary School, Walsall

Love

You put a smile on my face when you said I love you.
You opened your arms out towards me,
I blushed and I rushed towards you.
I came in your arms and you slowly whispered
I love you,
I will fight for you,
I will give up my life for you.
You sang a poem which started off with . . .
Roses are red,
Violets are blue,
Sugar is sweet,
Just like you.

Hannah Qaiser (12)
Abu Bakr Primary School, Walsall

Beauty Of Nature

Have you seen the beauty of nature?
How cool and calm it is
Birds flying high
In the warm sky

The grass so green and soft
Plants growing fast
While the petals grow last

The trees, growing tall and tall
From its deep, deep roots
As its leaves sway from side to side
It brushes my skin really light

People making roads
With the new mode
Destroying what was once there
Making it all empty and bare.

Roqia Rais (12)
Abu Bakr Primary School, Walsall

Happiness Is On Its Way

Laughing and jumping with joy
Whilst skipping down the stream
With bells tingling through my ears
And a bright smile on my face as I celebrate
The blossoms fly by with a beautiful scent
Delightful I feel as the bright sun shines out
Happily I run as I find my way back home
Home sweet home
I open the door to find an enormous cake
Sniffing, licking my lips
Suddenly I hear a shout
'Happy birthday!'

Zaakirah Ammara Begum (14)
Abu Bakr Primary School, Walsall

The Beauty In A Special Friend

If there's someone you can talk to
Someone no one can replace
If there's someone you can call on when you're feeling down
That one person that can change that nasty frown

Friendship is a gift
It can't be bought or sold
Its value is far greater than a stack of gold
For gold cannot cheer you in the time of trouble
It has no ears, no heart to understand your sorrows

If there's someone you can laugh with
Someone you can count on
If there's someone you think of every day
As the year goes on
Then you are a very lucky person
For you've found your special friend.

Khadiza Begum (13)
Abu Bakr Primary School, Walsall

Make A Stand!

Black, white, yellow and brown
Why do people make others frown?
There are times we laugh, and times we cry
This is the truth . . . no lie
Racism has no partner or friend, it always plots to the bitter end
It has the meaning to divide the mind just as it has divided us through time
We might all take this as a joke, but it's a serious matter which people provoke
You are you and I am I
So let's spread our wings and begin to fly
Let's take a chance and make a stand
For there are those who still don't understand
Be the change you want to make
No matter how long the time takes . . .

Masuma Nurjahan
Abu Bakr Primary School, Walsall

My Brother

My brother is sweet
My brother is neat
He likes to climb a long tree

He wishes to have a house of toys
Like most boys
He also makes a lot of noise
He loves watching ROY
His favourite crisps are McCoy's

His best friend is Umair
They both have spiky hair
Their favourite fruit is a pear
They have dreams of becoming a millionaire

He loves his sister which is me
Because I saved him from a bee.

Ume-Ahmen Kauser (12)
Abu Bakr Primary School, Walsall

It's My Time To Shine!

Think about other people for once
You're not in the spotlight
Your opinions make my heart ache
This time I'm not going to let you screech over my voice

I'm going to be heard amongst the crowds
Everyone going crazy over my name
Mine, not yours
It's my time to shine

I may look like a freak
But you haven't seen the other side of me
You can gossip all you like
But my mind is focussed on the right.

Mariam Lorgat (12)
Abu Bakr Primary School, Walsall

My Everyday Life

Silence . . .
Time goes by
Tick tock, tick tock

Loudness . . .
Time flies by
Come back, come back

When I start to enjoy myself . . .
It goes away, goes away

This happens every day . . .
Yes every day, yes every day

I hope this doesn't happen again . . .
Not again, not again

For this is like my everyday life.

Mehak Muskaan Khan (12)
Abu Bakr Primary School, Walsall

Nature

There are birds in the sky
Flying high
The green grass, the blue sky
Colourful birds wandering by
The nature's sound hitting off the ground
The night sky falls
When the sunlight calls
The flowers are blooming
The creatures are consuming
At the end of the day
They all make their way
And once again darkness embraces us all.

Mysha Begum (12)
Abu Bakr Primary School, Walsall

A Game Of Emotions

Emotions, emotions, just get overwhelmed with emotions,
Sometimes hatred, sometimes happiness,
Sometimes anger and sometimes mixed.
Emotions, emotions, some people don't care about other's emotions
For them it's like a game of football
They just aim for their goals and don't care about people's emotions,
All they care about is winning the game.
Emotions, emotions, are really important,
You shouldn't play with people's emotions.
Happiness, happiness, can't be bought,
As people say, 'Money can't buy happiness.'
Stop, repeat and think – are you saying the right thing?
Will it affect the way someone acts?
Will it stop them from being themselves?
Emotions, emotions, that's just how it works.

Ruqayya Yaseen
Abu Bakr Primary School, Walsall

The Loves Of Nature!

Roses aren't always red
Violets won't always stay blue
The fear that you're burying deep
You'll know that it was always true

Voices stretch out
Loud enough for you to hear
It's something that you have dearly loved
And its sudden shock will make you fear

I can't begin to describe how
How yesterday changed to now
But when you have a fear so deep
You know that you'll lose all your sleep
Your fear for only you to keep!

Maleehah Idrees (15)
Abu Bakr Primary School, Walsall

The Wonders Of The Nightfall (What Makes Me Happy)

The moon is a white, bright light,
Such a beautiful sight,
The moon glistens in the dark,
As I skip through the silent park

The wind brushes against my face,
My pounding heart begins to race,
For I feel a shiver at the back of my spine,
Yet I remain quiet hoping I am fine.

I hear noises in the street,
Looking down at my feet,
I witness a creepy 'it'
As it disappears through the foggy mist!

Safa Zia (11)
Abu Bakr Primary School, Walsall

Expressing My Anger!

When I express my anger,
I usually scream and shout.
I can't control it, no I can't,
So I have to go out.

Looking at my mum,
Gives me control.
If I don't, my face goes numb,
To calm me down I have a roll.

This is what I do when,
I express my anger.
All I would say is that
I love my mum!

Fahamida Alam (11)
Abu Bakr Primary School, Walsall

Tell Me The Truth

Tell me the truth,
Oh Ruth, oh Ruth,
Did I swear, I just can't bear,
Tell me the truth,
Oh Ruth, oh Ruth,
Did I kill, I don't want a bill,
Tell me the truth,
Oh Ruth, oh Ruth,
Was it an obsession,
Or did I go through depression?
Tell me the truth,
Oh Ruth, oh Ruth,
Was it love,
Or was it closed with a glove?

Samirah Chowdhury
Abu Bakr Primary School, Walsall

Why Should I Care What People Think?

The wind was blowing away my conscience
While the lake glimmered in the bright coloured sun
I didn't really have the confidence
But I didn't stop trying to get what I wanted
My self-confidence grew upon me
I didn't know what to do
So I just went outside to see if the rain would make it all go away
As the days came closer I felt like I was going to die
But as the moment came
I knew this was it . . .
As it came to me I felt I could do this
Why should I care what people think about me?

Zainab Bibi (12)
Abu Bakr Primary School, Walsall

Death

As I saw you take your last breath
I knew you were quite near to death

As the tears tipped out of your eyes
I knew this couldn't be a lie

A lie that soon you would be gone
That's the day I cried a tonne

I cried and cried all day long
As I knew I wouldn't be able to stay strong

The day that I thought you wouldn't end
I didn't think that death was just round the bend.

Fozia Kauser (12)
Abu Bakr Primary School, Walsall

Baking Makes Me

Baking is where I can be myself
It shows my true passion in what I do
Experimenting with different flavours
Is what I love to do, it's true.

Baking is my escape to freedom
From reality and stress.
Away from people and problems
It's like I have fulfilled my quest.

Suhera Jannah (12)
Abu Bakr Primary School, Walsall

My Pets

I had a cat,
But not a bat,
My cat's name was Jinx,
But he's not a lynx.

I had a fish,
When he died,
I didn't eat him on a dish,
My fish's name was Freddy,
He had two friends named
Eddy and Teddy,
I tried to make this rhyme,
Well, I did this time.

Safa Mohammed (11)
Abu Bakr Primary School, Walsall

My Grandmother

She kept an antique shop or it kept her
Among apostle spoons and Bristol glass
The faded silks, the heavy furniture
She watched her own reflection in the brass.

And I remember how I once refused to go out with her
Since I was afraid
It was perhaps a wish not to be used.

Aisha Alam (14)
Abu Bakr Primary School, Walsall

Anxiety

Anxiety is a condition hardly seen by others, known but not seen nor heard
Panic attacks occur and no one notices they were there
Hyperventilating again but no one seems to care
I love to hate my anxiety, it is to blame for my socially awkward days
My stomach churns again, no way
Why me?
Why today?
I was having an OK day
My fears are irrational but they never go away
I know I will never be heard because anxiety is only a word to the people who
surround me
I know they will never fully understand me
I know I can never be normal so isolated and alone
I'm truly lost for words, how can I ever move on?
A teenager with anxiety, lost, confused, alone
Confined by darkness with no real home.

Jasmine Sewell (14)
Blue Coat CE Academy, Walsall

The Realisation For Living

It's a life of temporary destruction
With a permanent desire
To find life's realisation
And the answers we require
But the answers will disappear
And the truth is so clear
Follow the actual reality that you can see
This is a world of confusion
And all the peace has gone
Fate is our only option left
Everything else is wrong
Beauty is fake
The evil is real
No more mistakes
Don't know how to feel
A shadow of darkness
A blanket of hope
Nowhere to go
Happiness is delusional
Look at all the hatred
Failing towards the righteousness
Giving up on the justice
We have to find the beauty
Now before it's too late
We live for the sake of living
Surrounded by all the hate
But we can find a motive
A reason to be here
We can find the answers
Only by a prayer
But not to any God
One kept towards ourselves
We are number one
And the inspiration's all around
Look at the sunrise
How it opens a new day
Look at the smiling faces
As they run outside to play
Look at the hugs and the love

Feel the fur and the trees
Smell the grass, smell the earth
And how it needs to be seen
Look at the new sprout of life
And the sparkling and the wonder
If that's not a reason to smile
I can't find any other
We don't all have to frown
This life is real
It isn't any movie
If you choose what to feel
We are not drones
We are not controlled
We are passionate creatures
And this is our world.

Jessica Roe (14)
Blue Coat CE Academy, Walsall

◯ Mind Wars

I feel the ground beneath my feet
But nothing is fresh, nothing is sweet

The bullets that come back and forth
As we men huddle tight travelling north

We go far and wide mile by mile
With friends by me all the while

Surrounded by soldiers but my mind feels alone
I will wait for the time when I can return back home

We sing the songs of love and peace
And wait for the gun that brings our release

But Heaven and Hell are far, far from my reach
As the things I have done deserve no preach

For I am a night crawler and our minds see no freedom
Till our souls are clean and full of wisdom . . .

Neve Plumb (14)
Caludon Castle School, Coventry

Surprise Surprise!

I wish it would just go away
The thoughts at night
The beatings in the day
I wish I could put on a brave face, wipe away the tears
Stand strong against them
Eliminate all my fears
They crush my hopes and dreams
Put a hand deep in my soul
Choose my life path for me
As though I have no goal
They punish us every day, for just no reason at all
Just because of our religion
Always them standing tall
I wish it would all just stop
Go away and disappear
Just grind to a halt
And let my nightmares disappear
They mock my cries
Of desperation and pain
Don't give me water
Not even from a drain
They've been torturing me like hyenas
Circling around their prey
Their eyes filling with hunger
Every time floods stream down my face
And my mouth a desert of dust
With my legs like stiff planks of wood
I know they always said they would
I didn't know they were capable of inflicting that much pain and terror upon me
I shouldn't have been so naive and foolish
Should have seen the danger signs
The ones that flashed in my face
Every time I closed my eyes
Yet I ignored them and carried on
Now look what's happened. Surprise, surprise!

Callum Moran (12)
Caludon Castle School, Coventry

Death

Close one eye and hope
Hope her life won't stop
Hope her pain will go away
And she will live another day

Death is the Devil
The stairway to Heaven
Or Hell
Depends on what side you're on

She's lying there, all grey in the face
Her pain just doesn't seem to budge
I wish I could take the pain away
And have my nan back again

Why do the best always have to leave?
And the worst stay behind
The ones we love most
Disappearing under our feet

The sky is dark and gloomy
And will never brighten up again
When Nan wakes
The world will too!

Tears trickle down my face
As the heartbeat stops
The beat once as strong as a drum
Is now so silent you can hear a pin drop

Close one eye and hope
Hope her life won't stop
But now she's gone
Her pain has gone away
And she will live another day
Somewhere safe.

Lauren Kieran (13)
Caludon Castle School, Coventry

Food

We all enjoy delicious food
Makes us happy and fixes our mood
It's all about the juicy taste
Doesn't matter where the food is placed

A great dish, we should all savour
Eat slowly, as we taste the flavour
Choose our very favourite bean
Is it red or is it green?

Food can taste sour
Fruits are processed in a tower
Sometimes it is sweet
You should consider having a treat

Having fun eating your food
Well in that case don't go and get tattooed
Stay and wait for more to come
You will get it when you hear the beat of a drum

Tomatoes are fruit or they could be a vegetable
Some people think they're nice, others think they are terrible
No one is right or wrong
To cook they don't take long

Mothers suggests tomatoes but children usually disagree
Children think they're not good for anything apart from the knee
People either love or hate them
Even if you love them don't eat them after 10pm

We all enjoy delicious food
Makes us happy and fixes our mood
It's all about the juicy taste
Doesn't matter where the food is placed.

Xanthe Hives (13)
Caludon Castle School, Coventry

Fire Alone Will Save Our Clan

The moon was high that night
And yowls of fear broke out
Blood was spilled, lives were lost
But one cat stood out

Eyes full of fury
Tense with his claws out
He leapt into battle with a loud roar
But in the end he didn't make it out

Alone she sat on the rock
Staring into the stars
Another came up beside her
And mewed silent words
'Have you heard anything from Starclan?'
But the she-cat shook her head
The other answered solemnly
'Too many lives have been lost'

Suddenly a star soared across the sky
And both of the cats looked up
The cat that had shook her head
Suddenly brightened up
The other cat asked with question
'Spottleleaf was that a sign?'
The tortoiseshell nodded smiling
And mewed, 'Fire alone will save our clan.'

Hollie Weir (11)
Caludon Castle School, Coventry

Koinobori

Red, blue, green and black
The koi carp snake their bodies
As the soft wind blows.

Amy Hall (11)
Caludon Castle School, Coventry

YoungWriters

Celebrate

Everyone, everywhere, has a reason to celebrate and people who care about them,
They are surrounded by happiness and all things good,
We follow our dreams,
If they travel near and far,
They drop, they fade but they're always there.

We walk, we play,
And live to see another day,
We learn, we grow with what we follow,
They can be like a flower,
Full of meaning but with their secrets.

Today, tomorrow, we are followed,
We have friends that care,
And enemies that don't,
And for that reason I thank you.

You're there for me,
I'm there for you,
We get better when we're together,
We grow together,
We learn together,
When you laugh, I laugh,
When you cry, I cry,
No one can compare to you!

Samantha Stoney (13)
Caludon Castle School, Coventry

The Ordinary, Humble Leaf . . .

The ordinary, humble leaf,
Unnoticed by even the most observant and appreciative of eyes,
Each shaped and coloured uniquely,
It can be as prickly as a hedgehog or as smooth as rubber.
Fluttering in the whispering wind like a butterfly,
It overwhelms with its revitalising, uplifting scent.

When a drizzly, misty, cloudburst of showers plunges,
The sincere, reliable leaf serves like an umbrella for one of nature's creations
– life,
Guarding and shielding them from these harsh, strident spears.

When the shimmering sun radiantly blazes its jubilant beams,
The simple leaf sensibly yet honourably hides anxious, defenceless prey,
From gluttonous, callous, merciless predator and vice versa.
As leaf itself is cleverly, cunningly camouflaged behind an anonymously-
arranged, anticipating army of pointed blades.

When autumn arrives,
The modest leaf reaches its last sorry day.
Cascading south off a now abandoned tree into the chalky, dusky earth like an
elegant, graceful feather off a fine, angelic bird in flight,
To be heartlessly trampled on by laughing miniature feet.
Crunch – the agonising sound of its last torturous words,
The ordinary, humble leaf.

Simran Rakkar (12)
Caludon Castle School, Coventry

Dystopian Poem

The sun descends into the inviting embrace of the clouds
The whole world is swallowed in the observing of chaos
Broken street signs swing to the rhythm of the cracked lamp post bulbs
What should be done?
Why am I still alive?

Kai Phillips (12)
Caludon Castle School, Coventry

My Birthday

Oh I can't wait for that special day
I have waited for 365 days
This moment has finally arrived
Just one more sleep
My heart is deep
I feel so magical inside
I wake early to see the clock
Ringing, *tick, tock, tick, tock*
As soon as it strikes eight o'clock
I simply can't wait
I rush out of bed on the dot . . .

On the old wooden table
There it lies
Glowing, beaming into my eyes
My very own journal
Not just any journal
But my great grandad's journal
It's dark blue with his initials engraved
I open the padlock with his special key
I turn the first page
It's a secret letter just for me.

Jeevan Saira-Dhadda (12)
Caludon Castle School, Coventry

A Dystopian Poem

As the day begins the people are working
To a day of trying to obey the rules
The odd one or two committing crimes where the only punishment is death
A hero rises like lava from a volcano conspiring with rebels
By night a government treating the villages like peasants burning houses
The hero rising from the ashes, discovering places and weakness throughout
the government, spotting the evil within them.

Conor McGuire (12)
Caludon Castle School, Coventry

My Life

My name is George, I'm 11 years old
I have autism but autism doesn't have me
I like learning and I try my best
But there are lots of people and noises which don't help me progress!
I like building things and designing cars
In art they want us to draw a vase
Maths I like because it's numbers and figures
But I like to make my friends laugh and giggle!
In PE it's always games with balls
But I don't like playing football outdoors
I don't like change it makes me feel strange
But the phoenix suite is my favourite place
Cars and Pokémon are my favourite things;
I really like it when I win!
This poem is about me so please take heed;
I don't really like to read;
Unless it's books about cars or Minecraft
But lots of people think I'm daft
My name is George Helliwell
I'm 11 years old
This is my life, you have been told.

George Helliwell (11)
Caludon Castle School, Coventry

Dreaming A Dream

Dreaming a dream you wish could be true
Dreaming a dream you would give anything not to
Dreaming a dream about what you love the most
Dreaming a dream about what scares you the most
Dreaming a dream that makes you wake up in laughter
Dreaming a dream that will make you cry after
But after all is said and done a dream is just a dream.

Zoe Lorraine Mai Brock-Turner (12)
Caludon Castle School, Coventry

Winter, Winter, Winter

Energetic whooshing, whirling winds
Swiftly swooping you off your feet
Plummeting raindrops at high speeds
As rapid as a cheetah
Devouring its mouth-watering juicy prey

Winter, winter, winter, it's trembling with cold
Diamond flakes of snow steadily drifting
To the crystal clear fresh blanket
Whilst you wrap yourself in a comfortable, cosy, velvety blanket
With a soothing beverage

Winter, winter, winter your body continues to quiver
Yet dismal atmosphere creating dull emotions
Snow, rain relentlessly falling from skies
Like cats and dogs
Banging on rooftops disguised like a herd of monkeys

Winter, winter, winter, enough noise, I need to sleep
Winter, winter, winter, full of bitter shivering weather
Winter, winter, winter, bring back the scorching calm sun
Winter, winter, winter you're not a wonderland!

Nawfal Hassan (14)
Caludon Castle School, Coventry

Humilitas

Flowers in the meadow
Hear the waterfall run
Children laughing, playing, smiling
Having lots of fun

Happiness shouldn't cost
A simple smile should warm a person's day
When the sun is shining
Go out and play.

Ana Maoudis (11)
Caludon Castle School, Coventry

We Talked Every Day

I met you that day
We were inseparable
We talked every day

We were only eight
We thought we were forever
We talked every day

We did everything
No one would get in the way
We talked every day

You met that one guy
You would never forget him
We talked every day

You spent time with him
My heart was smashed on the floor
We talked every day

We now never speak
We fought like wild cats and dogs
We were torn apart.

Jessica Hunter (13)
Caludon Castle School, Coventry

Why Me?

Why do I have to live in this horror?
Why do I need to be like everyone else?
Why do I have to be independent?
Why do I have to put up with them?
Why can't I express myself?
Why can't people see the real me?
Why am I misunderstood?
Why can't I be me?

Sonia Fard (12)
Caludon Castle School, Coventry

Dreams, Fantasies And Ideas

Dreams, fantasies and ideas
They're all in my head
Ideas to create
Fantasy to have fun with
And dreams that come true
Imagination is controlling me
Maybe it's real what I see
Drams, fantasies and ideas
What to make
My head reels
I know
I will create a game
With my dreams, fantasies and ideas
Testing my imagination
As I play and create
Roaming around in cyber space
I never get bored
Through the creative atmosphere I go
To a new world called dreams, fantasies and ideas
All inside a little black box.

Danaan Breslin (12)
Caludon Castle School, Coventry

Little Me

L ittle me
I just can't see
T his just isn't right
T oo fragile to be who I want to be
L et's just get over it so I can be free
E ven you can't see what it's like to be me

M e, it's just me, can't you see
E verybody just leave me be.

Megan Blake (12)
Caludon Castle School, Coventry

Fluffy Companion

Dogs, you are the best
Let's put it to a test
Fluffy, cute and cuddly
You make me feel bubbly
You deserve a treat
Maybe some juicy meat
When you wag your tail
It never fails
When you look up to me
It fills me up with love and glee
You sniff around looking for goodies
You will always be my four-legged buddies
I couldn't ask for more
Because you know I adore
I love it when you play
I can tell it makes your day
With your ball and your bone
You would never moan
We go everywhere together
And it will stay like this forever.

Amrin Dulai (11)
Caludon Castle School, Coventry

Alone . . .

In the evening when the candle light is lit
All alone I silently sit
Watching the hours go by
I try not to cry
I've survived through thunder and sunlight
All alone in one fortnight
Please let someone love me till May
I deserve more than to just look at the trees all day.

Olivia Grace Davies (12)
Caludon Castle School, Coventry

Ode To Dance

Dance is my muse
My rhythm and blues
I move to the beat
I dance with my feet
Life is a fiddler and we all must dance
It puts us in an elegant trance

You are a meticulous piece
You are my greatest caprice
Dancing in the rain
I can release my pain
From tap to ballet
I dance all the way

The magnificent time
It's me in my prime
I dance to the music
I could never refuse it
The beauty of art
Forever I will play my part
And dance.

Olivia Protheroe (13)
Caludon Castle School, Coventry

Love

Love your family
Love is where you pick them up when they fall
Love is when you care for them
Share with them and treat them fairly
Love is where you put others' needs before yours
You will not ask for something in return
Even though they change
Like the weather
Love your family more than ever.

Molly Bayliss (11)
Caludon Castle School, Coventry

Suffering Not Just Physically But In The Intellect As Well

Suffering not just physically but in the intellect as well
Orphans: lost, confused and alone
Who will care for them?
Staring into their eyes is like staring into a never-ending abyss of pain and torture
Agony fills my veins as my body is filled with excruciating pain
Mortal terror attacks my heart
Staring into the evil, cold hearted and merciless night sky
Sends out a horrible chill from my petty soul to my head
Knowing they're alone out there
No roof over their heads
No food to keep them healthy
And worst of all, knowing there's no one to love or to care for them
I feel as if I'm being locked in a never-ending carnage leaving nothing but despair in my empty heart
Tears fill right up to the brim of my eyelids overflowing with misery
I'm trapped; I can't help them
I'm just a kid . . .

Shaan Singh Rana (12)
Caludon Castle School, Coventry

Training

Training, training for a place
But still there's no start
My mind a fury of bubbles
Surrounding me all over the place
Watching the people pass by
I'm lost in my mind amongst the sky
Focussed on my future ahead
Learning day in day out
Training, training for a place.

Rhys Henton (11)
Caludon Castle School, Coventry

Poppies

The poppy I wore
Marching to the war
Waving goodbye on the way

The poppy I wore
Marching to the war
Just like the ones that survived
They survived the yellow clouds
They survived the men
And they survived the shells

The poppy I wore
Marching to the war
Just like the ones where I lay

The poppy I wore
Marching to the war
The same as the ones that are still growing today

Not just for me
But for everyone like me
The poppy is what keeps us alive.

Nathan Roper (13)
Caludon Castle School, Coventry

Runaway

You didn't tell anyone you were leaving
But it's time to sacrifice a lot because nothing around here seems appealing
But maybe you'll come back another day
When the young kids have put the knives away
But if not you might write a letter
Wishing that things will get better
But let's tell the truth, it's not going to change
Because everyone is stuck in their same old ways
So for now I'm just going to run away.

Maria Wilson (14)
Caludon Castle School, Coventry

Emotions Of Being A Teenager

Sometimes I feel sad
Sometimes I feel mad
Sometimes I feel blue
Sometimes I feel clueless
I'm an emotions wreck
I'm an emotional mess

Am I changing
Or is my happiness fading
I can't live like this
It's making me sick
What is this feeling
My heart is just peeling

I feel alone
If I'm ignored
This normally happens when I'm bored

Why are these the results I get
Because it's making me a living wreck

Am I an emotional teenager?

Ashley Prabhakar (13)
Caludon Castle School, Coventry

The Wave Of Dreams

The sun above fills my heart with joy.
I hear a seagull above and watch as it skims the sea in search of a catch,
I grab my bodyboard as the sand beneath my feet tickles my toes.
My pace builds up as I run towards the turquoise waves,
Suddenly the cold water reaches my skin as the spray hits my face like a cold shower.
I wait patiently for the wave of dreams, now the right time has come.
Like a dolphin I ride the wave towards the golden sand.
The seagull above now has his catch and I have ridden the wave of dreams.

Christian Mason (12)
Caludon Castle School, Coventry

What Makes Me Mad!

Something which makes me very angry
Something that makes me want to scream
Is that children are being used as slaves
You're probably asking, 'What does that mean?'

Well this is what this vile crime means
It means children have to work and get beaten
Even though they mean no harm, and they just want to live
Let me tell you this happens more than you think, I mean it could be your friend Ben

It could happen down your road but you wouldn't know
This is because these people are very sneaky and sly
If you do think this is happening don't be a coward
What you need to do is say goodbye

Goodbye to child slavery
Goodbye to being mean
Goodbye to horrible beating
Just let them be a normal teen.

Chris Lancaster (13)
Caludon Castle School, Coventry

The World Is A Terrible Place!

The world is a terrible place, riots, war and pollution
No one is safe here, no one in this terrible world

Riots on your doorstep, poor men on the floor
Pollution from the filling cars, riots everywhere

The world is a terrible place, riots, war and pollution
No one is safe here, no one in this terrible war

Extinction far away, polar bears dying out
The world is a terrible place, riots, war and pollution
No one is safe here, no one in this terrible world.

Georgia-Mae Flint (12)
Caludon Castle School, Coventry

Nature

Trees dance in the gentle breeze
Whispering to each other in the approaching moonlight
Beautiful flowers wave goodbye
As the sun floats down the horizon

Nocturnal animals breaking away from
Their beloved nests
Roaming the streets
Before hiding away from human life

With the streets as empty as the cloudless sky
The views are quite amazing!

Before dropping litter think
Of how it affects the
Natural beauty of our environment
Just put down your phone
For a second
Take in all the spectacular views
The majority of our world take for granted!

Erin Elliott (12)
Caludon Castle School, Coventry

Time To Escape

This faction is the land of hell, blood and fire and dread
If you step outside the gates you will certainly be dead

To get out, you need to think fast and smart and be quick at your escape
If you escape, it is not over, the hounds will hunt you down and gobble you up
like a grape

When you finally get out of all the pain from your faction
To keep alive, survival is your one and only option

Do not let the wild animals get you and kill you on the spot
Or rip you up and leave you at the bottom of a ditch to rot.

Lewis Bird (12)
Caludon Castle School, Coventry

Football On Match Day

Shouts from the stands
No doubts from the players
Which team will win
As the whistle goes
Nobody knows
What's going to happen
The ball goes boom
The manager hides in gloom
1-0 is the score
The fanfare singing praises
To the well-known faces
Players sweating
Dodgy fans betting
The ball is given a fling
The bar starts to ping
It hits the post
The final whistle blows
The winning team goes.

Arvin Corotana (12)
Caludon Castle School, Coventry

Guitar

Oh guitar
When playing you I get sore fingers
I am learning uplifting music
I enjoy playing music that makes my heart race
Learning chords is tough but fun
Music makes me feel like I'm a free spirit
Repeating music again and again
Until it's perfect
Oh guitar my musical friend
Thank you for being here with me.

Christopher Sollis (12)
Caludon Castle School, Coventry

A Dystopian World

The world seems dead and silent,
Abandoned buildings are starting to fade away into the darkness of the city,
The street lights that were shining as bright as the sun have started to darken
like the night sky,
My tears come falling down my face like a waterfall,
I miss everyone madly,
The children's laughter and the adults' loud shouts,
I wish very hard that everything could go back to normal,
I can only imagine the misery the people would have felt to see the city like
this,
How the soft sounds of the animals could be heard from miles away,
To the sounds of people screaming about their appearance,
I wish really hard that I could change things,
But then I come back to reality,
If only the rest were here,
The city would be shining as bright as the stars,
People would be laughing with happiness,
And people would actually start to care about other important things.

Maariyah Ahmed Butt (13)
Caludon Castle School, Coventry

You . . .

You scare me and you boss me around
You bully me when no one's around
You scare me and you throw me around
You should stop or you'll be put down
You're not fair and you're not right
I should tell someone but you might fight
You're not fair, you're never nice
It needs to stop, it can't last my whole life
You scare me and you boss me around
You're such a bully, people like you shouldn't be around.

Mia Shaw (11)
Caludon Castle School, Coventry

My Poem

I gaze from my perch on the hilltop at the rubble and destruction
Partly decomposed body parts are scattered here and there between fallen structures and landmarks
While smoke billows from a burnt down house
The last embers, much like the last glimpse of hope
Attempt to soar to the sky
But are soon all burnt out
Tears well up inside of me as I remember what a beautiful world this once was
The flowers in the meadows, the birds singing happily
All blown away instantaneously
Gone
Discarded slips of paper dance in the wind past frames of houses, shops and once mighty skyscrapers
All brought down spontaneously
As the paper floats past the last reminders of life and civilisation
I force myself to leave those wonderful memories
And come to terms with what the world is now
A barren wasteland.

Luke Glenn (13)
Caludon Castle School, Coventry

My Life

I am trying to escape
But I can't leave this cape
It won't let me go
I don't want to be part of the show
No one has my back
They just let me suffer
They throw me away
They don't let me stay
This is my life
Just end it with a knife.

Larghon Safi & Kordell (12)
Caludon Castle School, Coventry

The World

I wish the dove flew around the world
I wish it danced and twirled
I wish for the rose
I wish we could feel the love from out head to our toes
The humans are as violent as fighting bears
There is no one who cares
In this world there is only hatred
Bit like the girl I last dated
It wasn't nice
She only ate rice
So we never got along
But she sang a great song
Enough about me
Find out about me on the BBC
(Anyway . . .) This world is coming to an end
Just like the end of any trend
This is all I have to say
Hope I didn't offend you in any way.

Vipul Jose (12)
Caludon Castle School, Coventry

Summer In Peace

Flowers shining bright in the exquisite sky
Blooming petals rushed away from the calm wind
Sun sparkling in the great tree of peace
Bird singing as loud as a roaring lion
Flowers shining bright in the exquisite sky
Glory of happiness everywhere you glance
Summer has come warm and cosy
Heat surrounding you like a ghost of you
Hear the beautiful sounds of summer in your sharp ears
Glory of happiness everywhere you glance.

Qaidjouhar Adamjee (12)
Caludon Castle School, Coventry

Red Dyes

As the cold breeze washes my face from the day before
The dark smoke begins to form in the sky
The battlefield which was yesterday our stand
Is now a museum of ashes
Which still remember the cannon shots
Then there are the flags
Dyed with red dye, and our sacrifice

Burned barrels and tables
Grey like the sky
Surround me
And what was once my people's pride
Shown by the flags
Dyed with red dye, and our sacrifice

The revolution of the people has begun
And the days of old are nearly gone
Yet we still wait until the flags rise
Flags dyed with red dye, and sacrifice.

Aleksander Wroniak (13)
Caludon Castle School, Coventry

Predator

An eccentric atmosphere
Plagued with fear
Bullets flying overhead
'Keep your head down,' that's what I said
Filled with fear and desperation
I look to someone for inspiration
The whole world stood still
He was going to kill
I look into the eyes of my predator
His pupils fixated on mine
I think it's my time.

Jayan Bhambra (13)
Caludon Castle School, Coventry

Drowning

All around me darkness of the sea
Bubbles rise around me as I frantically try to swim to safety
I feel Death creep upon me
Drowning, drowning, drowning

All I can see is the navy of the azure ocean
No boats sail above me
No sea life swims around me
Drowning, drowning, drowning

My eyes are stinging with sea salt
My arms are getting tired
My legs are starting to ache
Drowning, drowning, drowning

I feel my lungs tighten
I must let go
I have to
Drowning, drowning, drowning.

Charleigh Gillies (11)
Caludon Castle School, Coventry

Music Is Always There For You

It speaks of happiness, of joy and not of fear
Music can be loud like storming thunder
Taking over every emotion in your body
Music can be soft like calm, peaceful souls
It speaks of happiness, of joy and not of fear

Music will always be there for you
Music is a way to express yourself
You can be inspired and saddened
When you have no one to go to music will be there for you
It comforts you when you're feeling down
Music will always be there for you to help take off pressure.

Ricky Nandha (12)
Caludon Castle School, Coventry

Pollution

Pollution rising in the sky
People hate the place walking by
It's about time to turn the bend
For all this pollution to end

Animals are losing their homes
To make way for buildings with domes
What message do we have to send
For all this pollution to end

We're all guilty we must confess
Guilty of making such a mess
It's time for action, find a friend
For all this pollution to end

If we don't act the world won't last
Breathing fresh air will have long passed
This is the message that I send
For all this pollution to end.

Anthony Nghiem (12)
Caludon Castle School, Coventry

Chelsea

C helsea are part of a fierce title race but the question is, can we win?
H elp is on its way in the form of Colombian winger named Juan Cuadrado
E veryone is tipping Chelsea to win the league
L osing the likes of Andre Schurrle to Wolfsburg and Mohammed Salah
    to Fiorentina may have an impact on our season
S o hopefully we can perform to our best and silence the critics
E ven Manchester City manager Manuel Pellegrini tips us to victory
    in both the league and European competitions
A gain comes January, the time where the best teams around the world
    knuckle down and try their best, so with that being said,
    come on you Blues, let's make a pact to be England's best team.

Sean Robert Evans (11)
Caludon Castle School, Coventry

We Are Dissimilis

We failed the test
We're inconclusive
That's what they say . . .
Inconclusive – now which way . . .

We run, we hide
We protect ourselves, we protect others
We fight, even when we can't anymore
We are Dissimilis

We keep in secret from the others
We're not like them
You hunt us down one by one
We're always a step behind
We are Dissimilis

We have no specific faction
We want no specific faction
We are Dissimilis.

Jade Hands (13)
Caludon Castle School, Coventry

War Is A Sin

Showers of bullets glide through the sky
Todd hurt his knee . . . just leave him to die
Rats that scavenge hunt for blood
They don't have feelings, give them a thud!
Letters to loved ones . . . if they pass
Forever lying in the grass
Life is a blessing, war is a sin
Can't ever forget all the things I did
They will be nightmares forever told
These are my memories and they can't be sold.

Jodie Phipps (13)
Caludon Castle School, Coventry

Your True Friends

Your true friends will always stay in your heart
No matter what happens, even if you're apart
They are there for you in times of happy and sad
They make your worries feel not so bad

Your true friends will always share your smile
With giggles and laughter for a long time
It's as if they can almost read your mind
With thoughts and ideas of the same kind

Together we dance and joke around
Probably making lots of sound
Having sleepovers up till dawn
Always giving us a yawn

So that is what a true friend is
Someone to share your smiles and tears with
So don't worry you don't need to hide
Your true friend will always be by your side.

Hannah Parkes (11)
Caludon Castle School, Coventry

Hope

A dark smog of misery blocks out the rays of happiness
Misery, despair, sadness and loss
Death, an everyday occurrence

The winds of change start to blow
The healing sands of time push the clouds away
The fabric of doom tearing apart . . .

A ray of light bursts through
Cleansing the world
Joy and happiness throughout the land.

James Harvey (12)
Caludon Castle School, Coventry

Death And Love

Love is so warm and sweet
So wonderful and good
Love can mean anything in the world
In life it means you are one with another

Love means you would spend your life with another
And love throughout those long years
And be loved back
But have you ever thought of death?

Death is the ending of love
But the beginning of another love
One you cannot see or hear
But will always be there

Death is so very cold
The opposite meaning of love
But yet they both mean
Being together with a loved one.

Leah May McGuigan (13)
Caludon Castle School, Coventry

Chocolate

C reamy, hard, soft but always sweet
H olding a love for us, never declaring a defeat
O h lovely chocolate, you are the best by far
C an't even be beaten by a fast car
O h no I don't want to imagine it without you
L ovely caramel is like tasty goo
A te you last night
T ook you in with one big bite
E at you every day all day, please don't run out day by day.

Ravi Tugnait (11)
Caludon Castle School, Coventry

⊛ Industria Poem

The world is ageing, and times are changing
Countries fight, all through the night
Children cry and parents die
No one is safe in this world of war

World leaders battle
City buildings rattle
Extremists loom large

But it's not all doom and gloom
As a new year begins to bloom
New advances in technology are made every day
Children in the streets begin to play

Even in this world of war
We are still at peace
We make new friends every day
With the people whom we meet
We choose not to fight, but to greet.

William Harvey Cowen (13)
Caludon Castle School, Coventry

◯ Dystopian World

D anger surrounds you everywhere
Y ou see someone in the corner of your eye
S imilar people surround you
T he walls seem to be closing in
O ut of the blue, an arrow zooms past
P inpointing the dangers
I nteresting things
A nimals are strange and weird
N ever trust anyone in a dystopian world.

Dilan Dusara (12)
Caludon Castle School, Coventry

I'm So Lucky To Have A Friend Like You

My friendship is great
My friendship is nice
I'm so lucky to have a friend like you

You take care of me
Stand up for me
You are there for me
I'm so lucky to have a friend like you

If others could see what you do
Then you have the world as a friend
Take a look, a look at my friend
See past the badness and into the goodness
If you can you'll have a new friend

I did that and it was a happy end
I'm so lucky to have a friend like you.

Jade Skelton (12)
Caludon Castle School, Coventry

The Winter Fright

Embers glowed softly in their dim light
Gazing round the room I greeted a sight
Bombs dropped simultaneously, *boom*
Was this really doom
Outside the snow fell, a blanket of white
This had to be a winter fright.

Karam Heer (11)
Caludon Castle School, Coventry

Why

Bombs fired around the place
Not a place to raise a kid

Stay out the way or you
Could end up in a bad way

Why do we do this?
For fun, for payback, what?

Nobody wants to live here
No more, it's torture

All you do is fight, work, fight, work
No sleep and no food. Why?

Why do we do these things
For fun, for payback, for what?

We wear a poppy to remember those
Who died but do we really mean it?

Taylor Leigh Byrne (13)
Caludon Castle School, Coventry

Snow

Falling through the sky I see,
Falling all around me.
Everywhere I look it's there,
A sheet so fair.
Snowmen I find,
Standing behind.
Lots of other people,
Snow was even on a steeple.
Snowballs flying in the air,
All people could do was watch and stare.
But then when it's gone,
Life goes on.

Ben Carr (11)
Caludon Castle School, Coventry

Bang Bang

Bang, bang
Another one's gone
Bang, bang
Is it me that will be next?
Bang, bang
The next shot could kill me
Bang, bang
One bullet could kill me

Bang, bang
Another body below me
Bang, bang
Will I make it through just another day
Bang, bang
Sound deafening my ears
Bang, bang
It's my turn, I'm gone.

Billie-Marie Ceairns (13)
Caludon Castle School, Coventry

Express

Darkness can overwhelm you, take over
It can have a strong emotional effect
Being depressed, sadness, dark thoughts
Covering you like a shroud

Don't look at the sea of trouble
Overcome the darkness, climb the troubles
Knock down the doors of sadness
Do not hide behind walls of depression
Strike down on your worries with great vengeance and anger
Channel the frustration to thought
Don't shout, don't hide
Come out from the darkness.

Ben Walmsley (11)
Caludon Castle School, Coventry

Blue Eyes

I saw her standing there
With her long blonde hair
Her eyes were gleaming blue
She's prettier than I knew
As she pulled out her lip-gloss
She saw me staring across
I glanced up at the skies
And thought, *how I love her blue eyes*

I saw him standing there
With his chocolate-brown hair
His eyes were sparkling blue
I hoped he'd noticed mine too
I pulled out my lip-gloss
As he was staring across
I glanced up at the skies
And thought, *how I love his blue eyes.*

Sabrina Lourenco-Arshad (12)
Caludon Castle School, Coventry

Journey To The Heart

Early morning sunrise
Cheek to cheek
All day splendid smiles
Make the heart aware of the emotions ahead
The hunger desire of passion
The heart must be fed

Simple words of love merely spoken
Just like magic
You leave their hearts wondering what happened
Whether it's roses or a dinner for two
For it might be the actions of love that say
'I love you.'

Reece McCook (13)
Caludon Castle School, Coventry

Dark Dull Dystopia

How would you feel if you were trapped
In a world so dark and dull
All you had to do was adapt
To the boring lifestyle that you were living
The things people would say would be so deceiving

How would you feel if you were
Never made to be good enough?
Always felt like you had to be the same
You'd always get the blame
And it would put you to shame

How would you feel if your life was controlled by someone else
Always being told what to do
I had a crew
They all flew
Away from this horrible world.

Chanell Grant (13)
Caludon Castle School, Coventry

Why Did You Go?

I stop
I just stare into space
Thoughts going through my head wondering why?
Just why did you have to go?
I wish, I wish more than anything that you didn't have to feel this pain
This brutal terror
Wishing I could turn back the clocks, make times as they were before
I can't do that
Then again, I feel your pain
I feel pain, the pain of losing you
Why did you have to go?
I try every day to forget, every day to get away from the pain
But all that I seem to think is why? Why you?

Tia Currall (12)
Caludon Castle School, Coventry

Unknown Soldiers

In this graveyard an unknown soldier lies
Flowers drizzled with tears from mothers' eyes
Here are many soldiers that surrendered
None of them were probably remembered

Brave soldiers gave up their arm and leg
Victory was the only thing they begged
War is wrong as it destroys families
People say they reunited the democracies

They all fought so we could be here today
They left their lives to fight so far away
These soldiers must have been brave
Worrying that they would end up in graves

We should be thankful for what they have done
Our lives and families is what they won.

Sahil Thakrar (14)
Caludon Castle School, Coventry

Current Affairs

Oh what a crisis
Here comes ISIS

Ebola is death
Death is Ebola
Although it might frighten
A cure is on the horizon

Is racism gonna stop
Or is a black boy gonna be shot?

Modern day slavery
We need more bravery
For people to come clean
And not be mean.

Kiran Singh Bahra (13)
Caludon Castle School, Coventry

Bottled Up

Silence
I'm floating
Floating alone, in a dark void
No one can hear me
I'm alone
Continuous whispers of childish laughter and angry demands filling my ears
Various comments such as, 'Stop trying,' or, 'You're useless'
I'm wishing to go that extra mile to stop this
But I can't
The dark void begins to drip black ooze
I'm now falling
Falling into the hands of darkness
I hit the ground
I wake up
Another rough night.

Emma Courts (12)
Caludon Castle School, Coventry

Bullies

Words can hurt me
I don't know why
All I want to do
Is just sit and cry

I hate it I really do
I just lose my confidence
Why oh why are they doing this to me?
Out of all of the people it has to be me

Nobody has asked me if I'm okay
I just feel like curling up
And sleeping till May
God please help me
I feel safe when you guide me your way.

Mollie Moore (13)
Caludon Castle School, Coventry

This Is The World We Live In

Look at what the police did
An innocent man killed
She was bullied so often
She overdosed on sleeping pills
What type of world do we live in?
Is it too late to change?
To rip out the hate
And start a new page
Look at what the police did
The right man freed
She told her mum and came clean
This is the world we live in
I would not want to change
This is the world we live in
On a new page.

Ella McKenzie (11)
Caludon Castle School, Coventry

Friendship

Friends love you, support you, care for you, believe in you
But that's not how I see it . . .

They use you, abuse you and spit you out
Like a bad taste in their mouth
You should always think twice
Before it's too late

You think they're nice
But really they're not your mate

Trust me, I've been there
It's not fair!

Why is our world such a nasty place?
Who gave them the right to judge our face?

Natasha Sharma (12)
Caludon Castle School, Coventry

A Dystopian World

A dystopian world
Being different is feared and hated
You cannot trust anyone, you only have yourself
A dystopian world
Full of darkness and dullness
Nothing in sight, but you must try to see the light
A dystopian world
Where fate is worse than death
Where everyone lives in fear, but happiness is near!
A dystopian world
A world where sunlight doesn't exist
Unless you make your own
A dystopian world
Where everyone is depressed
But be grateful and pray only for the best!

Zahrafina Saira-Dhadda (12)
Caludon Castle School, Coventry

It Hurts

Having a problem
No one can solve it
It hurts!

Hard to express your emotions
Feeling like people will judge you
It hurts!

Not knowing what's real
Hard to say how you feel
It hurts!

No one sees your pain inside
Like you're on a roller coaster ride
It hurts!

Lauren McGhee (12)
Caludon Castle School, Coventry

Teenager

Inside my head is a volcanic eruption,
My emotions are about to explode.
Outside is silent like still air,
On the land with the volcano nobody knows what is to come.

I'm at boiling point, fuming and frustrated,
While my dad's cheerful as usual.
'Being a typical teenager,' he would say,
He doesn't know how it feels as he's an adult.
It was millions of years ago when he was a teenager,
Dinosaurs ruled the earth when he was my age.

I want to play on my iPad,
But my dad wants me to do my homework.
Homework is pointless, why bother?
Like it helps in life!

Emily Allman (13)
Caludon Castle School, Coventry

Breaking Rules

Life is too short
Break the rules
Don't listen to what they say
Don't be afraid to break the rules
Change the rules
Bend the rules
'Cause I destroy the rules
Society is messed up
Too many rules, no space
To liberate
Exaggerate
Contemplate
Break the rules.

Sophie King (13)
Caludon Castle School, Coventry

Love At First Sight

You stared at me
I stared at you
We knew this was meant to be

You looked away
But I wasn't okay
I thought this was meant to be

I tried my best
But you're just like the rest
Then I realised it wasn't meant to be

You stared at me
I looked away
For now I knew you weren't okay

Love at first sight is not meant to be.

Kia Eyden
Caludon Castle School, Coventry

Looking For Love

Looking for love I see him right there
Looking for love with his lock of hair
Looking for love we would make a good pair
Looking for love I will treat him with care
Looking for love
I looked for love, I have cried a waterfall of tears
I looked for love, I have so many fears
I looked for love, it has been the worst year
I looked for love
Hoping for love there I lay
Hoping for love will it happen one day
Hoping for love will I stay
Hoping for love.

Suchita Patel (11)
Caludon Castle School, Coventry

Snow And Snowflakes

Snowflakes have their intricate design
Sparkling and glistening all the time
Cold to hold but soft to touch
Put some gloves on and fine to clutch

Imagine being buried in all that deep white snow
You would be freezing cold but wouldn't want anyone to know
Because they would start to scream and shout
And frantically try to dig you out

It's been long enough now so you start to shout
Hello up there please come and get me out
Once you're out snowflakes start to fall again
But the hole seems to still remain.

Kyra Maycock (12)
Caludon Castle School, Coventry

Ebola

I don't even know where to start
How does Ebola strike so hard?
Early signs like Malaria
We must fight to beat Ebola

The disease has now gone viral
I can't believe this is real
Aid has gone to Liberia
We must fight to beat Ebola

Fatality rate is so high
Only one in ten will survive
Donate to prevent Ebola
We must fight to beat Ebola.

Brindan Tharmaseelan (12)
Caludon Castle School, Coventry

Oh Chocolate

I care for you like my own baby
I treat you the same as I would a lady
You're so delicious I could eat you for breakfast, lunch and dinner
Because when I buy you I feel like a winner

So when I buy a bar
And start to unwrap
My heart starts pounding
Like rat-a-tat-tat

I like you melted
I like you solid
If someone tries to hurt you
They'll definitely get pelted.

Josh Coope (12)
Caludon Castle School, Coventry

Friendship

I feel like I have known these forever
Because we are always together
When I'm feeling down
They are always around

You've kept my secrets
For many years
When I need help
You're always here

I promise to always be here
Right until the end
You are all the true meaning
Of very best friends.

Ava Norma-Jean Bremmer (13)
Caludon Castle School, Coventry

Death Camp

Despair surrounds us everywhere
Evil people who just don't care
Amplified fear across the hours
That we will be next in the showers

Comrades all of us in this awful place
Hoping one day we will see a friendly face
Thousands of families ripped apart
Don't these people have a heart?

Soldiers walking around so brave
Throwing people into mass graves
Hope is dwindling at a massive pace
Auschwitz is an awful place.

Rebecca Lyons (14)
Caludon Castle School, Coventry

Me

My name is Mason
My age is twelve
No matter what, I will always be myself

I have autism
But it never gets the better of me
I have always managed to fit in with everyone else

When I am with my friends
I feel happy
Accompanied and safe
All I need to do is
Find my happy place.

Mason Hill (12)
Caludon Castle School, Coventry

Why?

What is wrong with the world?
People killing or seriously injuring another human
Can't we live in peace?
I bet in a million years time the human race won't exist because of other people mindlessly slaughtering other humans
How could you live with yourself after you'd killed or seriously hurt someone
It's amazing how people have the nerve to do it
Why would you want to kill someone or hurt them?
The world would be a better place without killing, shooting, hurting
Countries living in fear
People spreading terror
I wish it would all just stop!

Christie Horrillo (12)
Caludon Castle School, Coventry

A Teenager

You begin to be a teenager
Homework builds the blanket of pressure
The temptation of smoking gets bigger
Video games start to corrupt your being
You start to get in a habit of swearing
You begin to be a teenager . . .

James Tarancón-Byrne (11)
Caludon Castle School, Coventry

⚖ Emotions

Emotions are funny and sometimes unclear
One minute you're sad then the next you're full of cheer
Emotions are funny but sometimes awkward
One minute you're SpongeBob then the next minute you're Squidward
But emotions are a big part of our life
They control our happiness and our strife.

Aneesah Khan (11)
Caludon Castle School, Coventry

🕊 Best Friend

They come by chance, but stay by choice
You will smile every time you hear their voice
They will smile when you're smiling
And feel the ache you do
Because they're your best friend
And that's what they do!

Ellie Lawrence (12)
Caludon Castle School, Coventry

How Hard It Is To Write A Poem

I stare into the paper desperately
Trying to write a line or two
Quickly
My mind is blank
To be quite frank
Dot, dot, dot
That doesn't say a lot

How hard it is to write a poem
If only I knew
What I was doing
This is taking me forever to write
It gives me an awful fright

Sitting at my desk, my mind trembles
I can't think anymore
My thoughts start to crumble
The words in my mouth begin to jumble

My pen is going dry
Sizzling, sizzling
My brain is starting to fry

Oh how hard it is to write a poem
If only I knew what I was doing.

Nadim Hussain (15)
Jalaliah Educational Institution, Tipton

My Father

I'm glad you're my father
You're really the best!
You're one in a million
I am truly blessed

You pay attention to me
Listen to what I say
You pass on words of wisdom
Which help me along the way

You make my life much better
The best father I know is you.

Junaid Chomok
Jalaliah Educational Institution, Tipton

Football Fun

They like to kick a ball
When the crowd are high
Start to shout and call
Goal . . .
Offsides are hated
People's faces are painted
Come on Man U
They are beating you
If you can score this goal and the ball doesn't hit the pole
You could win!

The match is over
Planes hover around the stadium
People are jumping and screaming
Whilst the lights are gleaming
Bye-bye everyone
Thank you players we had
So much fun!

Nadeem Al-Hassan & Adam (12)
Joseph Leckie Academy, Walsall

Temperantia

A group of people
A group of friends
Promise to be there till the end

A bunch of tales
A bunch of lies
No matter how hard one tried

Then one by one it falls apart
Nobody actually takes it to heart

Then they apologise, all fake
Wondering whether to give or take

Being kind
I put it behind
Despite it all
My friends I call

Then once again
It comes to an end
I guess you're wondering
What comes next . . .

That's the part I do not know
All the feelings I can't show
All the worries in my head
I'll have to think about it
When I'm in bed.

Aisha Tahliil & Michaela (11)
Joseph Leckie Academy, Walsall

Anger

You creep up on me, like the cold
Slithering down my spine
Caging the warm heart inside of me
You turn me into something I am not

To block this rage
And break the cage
I have to try harder
Before my heart gets darker

There is no point in hoping
If I don't try
To beat this evil sin inside
You're burning inside of me and it's hard to control

You make me evil
Struggling to get out of your traps
They say patience is a virtue
But it's not as easy as it seems

Regretting taking the anger out on loved ones
I isolate myself from everyone
Cooling down in a dark room . . . all alone . . .

Khadija Khatun & Mahera Anjum (12)
Joseph Leckie Academy, Walsall

My Special Day!

Today is special
Can you guess what day it is?
I'll wake up early
I will be very noisy
Waking everyone up
Today is my special day!
I'll dress in my special clothes
And spend all my money
Go down to the shops
And come back for my party
All my family and friends
Here with my presents all for me!
Party time for me
Fresh cream cake, with a cherry on top, hmm so yummy
Dancing all the way
Can you guess the day?

Maham Javed (12) & Mandeep (11)
Joseph Leckie Academy, Walsall

Temperantia

Oh how I hate
The government
They're not great
I want to cover them in cement

They can't run the country
They can't run the schools
They're all a bunch of monkeys
They're all stupid fools

They're actually alright
They're not that bad
But boy oh boy
Do they drive me mad!

Louis Joseph Reeves (12) & Soger (11)
Joseph Leckie Academy, Walsall

It's Coming I Say!

It's coming I say
It's coming
The disease that has killed over 100,000 people
When people find out they've got it
They scream in agony all night long

Lots of people want to help and get rid of it
And some don't
Scientists working night and day to find a cure
But they don't succeed
But there are silly people out there, very silly
They laugh at it
And they make fun of it

What can we do?
What can we do?
It's coming I say, Ebola is coming.

Sohaib Ashraf (12)
Joseph Leckie Academy, Walsall

Eid Day

The best festival of all time
Everyone gets together down mine
Lots of delicious food to eat
Samosas, rice, jalebi and meat
It's Eid
Mehndi patterns all over my face
Wow! This mehndi really went to waste
Shivering in my new dress
But there's me still trying to impress
It's Eid!
Gifts and money for everyone
I love pass the parcel! Guess what . . . I won!
Make-up and jewellery all over me
Hey! Most of them were actually free!
It's Eid!

Nimrah Altaf, Aisha & Hina (12)
Joseph Leckie Academy, Walsall

My Mommy

You are so special
You mean the world to me
I know I annoy you
But that's just me

You've always been there for me
Since the first day we met
Even though I'm naughty
I'm still your little pet

I'll take you on a journey
You'll always be by my side
I love you to death
I'll never leave you behind.

Jamie Andrews (12)
Lyndon School, Solihull

New Moon – The Jump

I jumped . . .

The gravity pulled me down to the water
I was a leaf falling from a tree
The wind started biting at my skin
And every second I was getting closer to Earth
There was no turning back, there was no turning back

Head first I went under
It was more peaceful than expected
It was dark and I was surrounded by my thoughts and his voice
Edward's voice
He was angry at me
But the beauty in his voice
Stopped me from listening to the words that he said
I didn't care, I didn't care

The tide started to come in
And a flicker or orange passed my face
It looked like hair
Victoria's hair
Was she back to seek revenge because of her best friend James' death?
I didn't know, I didn't know

The tide got stronger every minute I thought about Victoria
I hit against the rock
Once, twice, three times
My lungs filled with salt water burning my throat
This is not what I imagined
My eyelids closed into darkness
I needed help, I needed help

Something grabbed me
Was it Victoria?
I tried to force my eyes open
Nothing happened
All I heard was a low voice, almost a growl
I recognised it at once
It was Jacob, my Jacob.

Orla Cullen
Lyndon School, Solihull

Billy And Lilly – My Favourite Dogs

You meant the world to me
You were my best friend
I hope you now can see
Our love will never end

I miss you dearly
I hope I'm doing you proud
I love you sincerely
I don't ever want to make you frown

Now, I have another best friend
However mine and your friendship will never ever end

You are so special to me
You always make me smile
You always run free
And make me run a mile

Our love will never end
You will always be by my side
You will always be my friend
I will never leave you behind

I love you so much!

Jodie Duffill (12)
Lyndon School, Solihull

I'm Lost

I woke up this morning
I felt different . . . It wasn't a good different either!
I hate everything right now, I don't know why

I walked in the bathroom
I grabbed a blade
I ran the silver thing through my skin and red poured out . . .
Seven times; it goes through

I tried to stop but I couldn't
It was hard
I was considering on . . . suicide
Bent, cracked . . . broken
Help me!

I hear the thundering of happiness in my head
But in other places I hear the pounding of depression
Heart aches, bones ache, everything flipping aches!
On Instagram I get hate for being an emo
I shouldn't but I do

Most girls seem to like Ed Sheeran and that
My taste is more Slipknot!
I get bullied every day of my life, I'm a mistake
I can't take this anymore!

Rachael Lane
Lyndon School, Solihull

Dear Brother

My favourite thing in the whole wide world
Remember you growing from a baby to nine years old
I know I can share absolutely anything with you
I find it funny when you step into my shoe
You will be the first movie I pick on a movie stack
I want to let you know I've always got your back.

Kaiya Antrobus (12)
Lyndon School, Solihull

Rugby

Rugby, listening to the smash of skin
As the ball goes high up
You can hear them call
As the ref blows the whistle
Sheer power from the pack
Pushing for the ball
As low as they can go

Seeing the mountains of men hit others
You can just feel the pain
On the line
Ball goes in, men jump for the ball
Off they go running at the speed of light
Down the wing
The crowd with tension
Will he make it or will he not
Bang!
The ball goes down with a thud
Now the crowd goes wild
Try!

William Clarke (12)
Lyndon School, Solihull

Stop

Stop bullying
It makes people feel alone
It destroys them from the inside out
Emotionally hurts them
Physically destroys them
They will never feel the same
Would you like it?
No
Then stop.

Sallyann Faulkner (12)
Lyndon School, Solihull

Dying A Hero

I'm running out
Everyone's staring at me
I'm feeling doubt
I take an arrow to the knee
I carry on running
I want to help my country

Everyone follows me
While I'm taking everyone on
I'm wearing armour
It weighs a ton
Everyone's on the floor
I think we've won!

Gallons of blood
Pouring out my knee
I die
But I helped my country!

Lewis David Barber (13)
Lyndon School, Solihull

Love Is Us!

You are my love
You are my everything
You are my shining star
You are my glowing heart
You sparkle in my dreams at night
I wanna hold you oh so tight

Love
Happiness
Surrounds us all
But mainly us
We will never fall.

Hollie Wadman (11)
Lyndon School, Solihull

Me And My Fabulous

My family
They always make me smile
Even though I'm sometimes in denial
My two big sisters
Can sometimes be cruel
And make me their mule
But know that I still love you
If you don't believe in angels
Then you haven't met my mum
My magnificent mum
You make me so happy
From before when I was in a nappy
To today in the morning
And hopefully for the future to come
Family is my everything
I love you with all my heart
And with my heart I knew you love me too.

Maariyah Shahid (11)
Lyndon School, Solihull

Facing It Alone . . .

It's never-ending
I can't take anymore
Threat after threat
Nobody knows except me
It's emotionally hurting me
It's physically breaking me
What have I done to deserve this?
It is terrifying
I can't control it
What should I do?
I hate facing it alone.

Megan Barton (12)
Lyndon School, Solihull

Sparta!

A solitary soldier of the battlefield
A whole army killed under his blade
Nerves like steel a sword of as thousand souls

In a box of tales that will never be told

Revenge on his face he stares at the opponent
300 men Vs the bloodthirsty Persians

Who will win?
Who will die?
He does not care as long as he dies in pride
He runs at the Persians, sword in hand
The battle must commence
There is no longer a law of the land

The screams of perishing men fill the air
The battle is over, the deed is done
There won't be a Persian left under this Greek sun.

Billy Gadd (11)
Lyndon School, Solihull

Feelings For You

I see your face every day but yet my feelings never change for you
You're sweet
You care
You are everything to me but yet you will never understand
How much you mean to me
Only if you could see what you mean to me
Only if you could see how much I care
No matter how far away you will always be near my heart
You're the spark in my heart
I wish I could explain
So I wrote this for all the people I love
Especially you.

Hannah Teal (11)
Lyndon School, Solihull

Equal

Some people don't seem to grasp
The simplest concept of them all
Equality means everyone is equal
Because we are all equal
We're not all the same
That is the amazing diversity of our kind
It's what makes us human
You might come under the rainbow flag
Perhaps the pink, white and blue
You can come from any corner of the globe
You can believe in your faith
You can be proud of your origins
We're diverse
It's what makes us human
Because equality isn't a disguise for discrimination
Equality means everyone is equal.

Connie Hammond (13)
Lyndon School, Solihull

Mom

I follow in your footsteps
Everywhere you go
You're the queen of my world
And I love you so

You work very hard
You never seem to rest
I never want to leave you
Because you're the best

You are so special to me
That will never change
So I hope you can see
I love you and you love me.

Lucy Thomas (12)
Lyndon School, Solihull

Young**Writers**

The Awoken Beast

A beast from Earth has risen
And will destroy everything in its path
The Earth's destruction has awoken
It kills animals for entertainment
Uses Earth resources for itself
And it's populated across the continent

The world's natural beauty
Consumed and destroyed by
A monstrous and murderous beast
And it thinks it's all fine

No one knows who this monster is
But it is right under their noses
You may think, *what do you mean?*
But it's you
Humanity is Earth's destruction.

Thomas Campbell (13)
Lyndon School, Solihull

Gaining My Pleasure From My Treasure

Oh dear Minecraft, when will I find a mineshaft?
I need to find my treasure, and as I dig and dig
I make the hole very big
My pickaxe is almost at his end
I dig a bit more, it starts to bend
Now I start to believe I am at my end
All I want is my beloved pleasure of finding my priceless treasure
As I see my gems I start to cheer
But really I should fear
This is a set up, as I am surrounded by TNT
I believe this is the grand for me.

Alex Philip Maine (13)
Lyndon School, Solihull

Greatest Mom

Strong and brave
Loving and caring
The greatest mom in the world
Loving and caring like no other
The greatest mom in the world
Warm-hearted like tea and biscuits
Mother and daughter relationship
Like two magnets
Greatest mom in the world
You're my fairytale queen
And I'm your princess
Nothing brings us down
Greatest mom in the world
Love you now
Love you always
Greatest mom in the world.

Holly Lewis (12)
Lyndon School, Solihull

Her Other Side

Like the demons that
Hide within her
She lurks in the shadows
Her incredible beauty fools
Her other side seduces you
But looks can be deceiving
Don't be fooled
Her enchanting looks
Conceal the darkness
Beware!

Yasmine Osborn
Lyndon School, Solihull

Humans

Bones breaking
Necks cracking
Brutal stabbing
Who are these beasts?
They inject and take blood
They force things into their throats
And then they gloat
To the world
We faint at the sight of it
We fight for the rights of it
Who are these beasts?
They stab and crack at those we love
And out of all of the above
Who are these monstrous beasts?
. . . Humans . . .

Samaa Altaf (12)
Lyndon School, Solihull

No Place Like Home

Sitting in the streets all alone
Got no place to phone
Children crying
At least somebody's dying

Hurt, father, mother, daughter, son
Look what's been done
Personality, spirit, self-control lost
All my life it's cost.

Akirha Lakisha Skeete-Simpson (11)
Lyndon School, Solihull

Give Back Something

Throughout my life you were there
Always by my side
Even though I never thought it
You were always filled with pride
I always used to take you for granted
But now I truly see
That I would never be here today
Without you caring for me
Now I am older
I still love you to bits
And I will forever
I want to give something back
For giving me the best gift ever
Life.

Rosie Johnson (11)
Lyndon School, Solihull

Soldier

Marching, marching, marching.
Preparing, preparing, preparing.
Ready, ready, ready.
Bang, boom, soldiers fight!
Soldiers wondered,
On the way there,
If it was their final fight.
With all his might,
Bright, bright red,
All over the wasteland.
With no haste the soldier
Got up and ran
To his mate,
Using all his pace . . .

Joshua Myers (12)
Lyndon School, Solihull

My Mom

You shaped me
You made me
Without you I wouldn't be me
You cried for me
You fought for me
I need you there with me
Although we may argue
Although we disagree
You'll never leave my side
I know that with certainty
Although we may fight sometimes
Although you may not see
I love you with all of my heart
I'd follow you through the galaxy.

Evie Croxford (11)
Lyndon School, Solihull

The Teenagers Of Today

Not feeling yourself
Empty, alone
People who care about you
But you push them away
But we are the next generation
Trouble-makers, brain-washers
Self-harming, ashamed about the way you look
Don't listen to them, you are perfect.

Rhiannan Brookes (11)
Lyndon School, Solihull

Mum

The one who loves you
Who can't stop loving you
She guides you through the good times and the bad
She never lets you down
You love her and she loves you back
Love
But through good times and bad times don't forget
She is your mum . . .

Jack Lane (11)
Lyndon School, Solihull

Life Through My Eyes

Footsteps creak, here they come
Screaming, crying, what's the point?
Punch, kick, bruises all around
Wanted to leave this burning hell
Blood drips from my hips
Depression hits me like a bat
Wanted to fly high but the happy angel fell to her fate.

Danni Lonsdale (12)
Lyndon School, Solihull

The Palestine Kid

I stand looking at what used to be my village
My home
My reality
Now all I see is war, blood and sadness
What the soldiers in the planes don't understand
Is this isn't a warzone
But it is my home.

Inam Hussain (12)
Lyndon School, Solihull

A Dream

Blazing through the dead barren land
Dreaming of a life living grand
Walls ahead standing strong waiting for the ball to land
Suddenly a rocket soars past the fortification of a defence
Rip, the net is torn
A goal is scored
The dream is slow approaching.

Joshua Trowman
Lyndon School, Solihull

Freedom

We have been more than successful as humans:
Tried so hard to earn something that was so easily snatched from our possession
Freedom

We might be free from the chains of our pigmentation
But we're still unable to believe in what we want
Freedom
We've made religion the problem with the world
People can't fly without fearing life
We cannot smell freedom until the day Mr Mohammad can board a flight without being double checked

We have used religion to justify terrible inhumane acts causing people to turn their backs on God
This is not freedom
Freedom is a flavour our lips have not yet fully tasted: only a sample
We've let religion put us in chains we claim not to have
How dare we say we have human rights, when we've allowed ourselves to become slaves to religion
We've let ourselves believe bad things can happen as long as it is in the name of God
We don't know freedom because we don't know the importance of life
Many people wake up to find out their loved ones have been killed in a terrorist attack
Many have become widows and orphans because of a person's beliefs, who they don't even know
And it's funny how the western world claims to have so much stability, yet is shaken by these acts and is easily put into unrest
This is not freedom
Freedom is still a dream we have yet to reach
And to our next generation we should teach
Freedom can't always be taken by loving speech
Sometimes things should be taken by force
Freedom.

Tanaka Jana
Lyng Hall School, Coventry

She

There's people out there living a lie
When all they do when they're alone is cry

They picked the sharpest object which then became their latest companion
Because who else can she turn to when she's being abandoned

She's trapped
Words stabbed

She's not herself anymore
But fighting against her own war

She's denied
She feels the divide

The hate has taken over her brain
Physically and mentally in pain

Her thoughts are full of negative
While her life could have been productive

Her confidence is gone
Death is drawn

Happiness and smiles are everything a person needs
But they continue to hurt her, even after she bleeds

Nobody cares, is what's she's thinking
That's what she's believing

What she doesn't know is that there's someone out there
Whose heart is pure and clear

But why should she trust that one person
When all her life she's been trusting, but they're just the same version

There's people out there
People who care
But all they hear is hate
So, it would be too late

Too late to take positivity into consideration
Not even using the famous alliteration
To live. Love. Laugh

The basic rights everybody needs
Having to fight, and . . .
To plead?

I'm going to end this poem, with this thought in mind
And remember, it never hurts to try and be kind.

Idora Musa
Lyng Hall School, Coventry

Bringing It Back

Nothing you can do or say will change me
Take my happiness away you can't
C'mon try and detach me
Once you do you'll be eating an ounce of beef
As well as choking on my wrath of insanity

For the past six years you did nothing but bully your way through my head
Like it's an open door
You walk in and take a part of me
Like it's free

I'm going to change my mood
This time I'm not in the mood
To deal with your mood

I've done nothing to you, but nope, you're still rude
I'm no longer in the mood

I'm finally changing my tone
I'm leaving don't ever call my phone

Goodbye.

Brandon James Brookes (14)
Lyng Hall School, Coventry

The Christmas Poem

The snow falls
On ice pools
The children have a snowball fight
The mothers worry about frost bite
Santa reaches his destination
So all the kids can have a celebration
People write about the night
When the stars were super bright

At the meal, we have a beer
We all get drunk, scream and cheer
We fill the turkey
With beef jerky
Your mum guards it like a knight
It is really tempting to have a bite

Christmas is over
The snow falls slower
No more turkey
And the outside is murky.

Ethan Gray (13)
St Benedict's Catholic High School, Alcester

Cold-Blooded

Cold veins
Red fists
Through cracks hearts and walls

Don't touch me

Aggressive he, broken me
Do I give rest or do I leap up for air

I never thought this would be true, is it?
Don't blame me
Do not convince me or yourself

My purity, gone
I was always the victim
You were never the innocent one

I'm hot blooded
My blood boils inside
Oh my anger
Oh my pain.

Sean Finn (14)
St Benedict's Catholic High School, Alcester

For The Love Of My Life

You are my sun, my moon
You're my words, you're my tune
My earth, my sky, my sea
You're everything to me
My love and affections
You are perfection

I think I love you
But it's just not right
That I'm dreaming of you
Every night.

Marco Bille (14)
St Benedict's Catholic High School, Alcester

Treasures Of Friendship

One of life's treasures is a friendship
A friendship for life
Insistent to have only one best friend
The title we may choose
The treasures do not mean as much to me
As your friendship means to me
All the frowns I've worn that you've turned into smiles
With feeling no shame or the blame
The darkest secrets are here, forever they will stay
I can't give you all the answers
But I can listen
Together we will search for a solution
I will never leave your side
Forever is where I will stay.

Cara McGhee-Browning (14)
St Benedict's Catholic High School, Alcester

Football Is The Best

The sound of the ball clatters as it
Hits your foot
When you throw the ball it
Scoots over my head like a
Comet in the sky
The adrenaline rushing through you
When you run and play the game
You kick it, throw it in the goal
You can win and you can lose
But your sportsmanship
Is what matters.

Andy McKeown (13)
St Benedict's Catholic High School, Alcester

Don't They Have A Right To Life?

Locked in cages
Taught to fight
Hungry for days
Don't they have a right to life?

What have they done to deserve such abuse?
The number of injustice we should try to reduce

Hunted to extinction
Denied a life they deserve
An unfair sentence
They are forced to serve

What have they done to deserve such abuse?
The number of injustice we should try to reduce

They are defenceless animals
Denied of aid
Continually mistreated
They are alone and afraid

What have they done to deserve such abuse?
The number of injustices we should try to reduce

We can make it stop
We can draw the line
For these vulnerable souls
Who are running out of time.

Rhea Boora
The Earls High School, Halesowen

Totalitarianism - Haikus

A terrible world
Full of violence and terror
Like the Underworld

There's no freedom here
Nor does privacy exist
Our deaths could be near

We stepped out of line
Then the explosives rained down
Dread ran up my spine

Oh, so much is lost
We are the death of ourselves
The world's cold as frost

Pity, it's all gone
Landscape, now piles of ashes
The sun never shone

Humans are ruthless
Causing so much destruction
The world now worthless

Was there any hope?
Any light to this dark place?
How did people cope?

Wing Suet Koon
The Earls High School, Halesowen

The Soldier Stood

And so the soldier stood
In memory of his friends who were lost in a blood wrenching war
He stood with only the sound of silence to remember the lost men and children
And the thoughts of grieving families who have no more tears left to cry
He thought of the children with no mothers
Who lie cold and alone at night
He thought of the widows who have no husband to tell them everything is OK
He thought of the soldiers who will come home to nothing but pain and loss
But most of all
He thought of the families who will never fully recover from darkness
The soldier remembered the frightful war
The thick mud, rotting bodies, lives being tossed like footballs
And the deadly night air which killed quicker than a machine gun
Even though he was English he went to visit the 'enemy'
As he knew all of them were like him
They too had lost family and loves ones
And so the old man stood and lay down a poppy
To remember these men and that they were here in a war
Over 100 years ago
They lost their lives to make our world a better place.

Sianan Conroy (12)
The Earls High School, Halesowen

A Day With My Mom

She would carefully tuck me into bed
She would pray so I had a pleasant sleep
And then she'd softly kiss my tiny head
Then after in the covers I'd count sheep

Come morning she would have breakfast prepared
She'd call from the stairs, 'Sufyan hurry up!'
For school she would make sandwiches with bread
With breakfast she'd give me milk in a cup

At home-time she'd be waiting with a smile
While she's driving we'd talk about my day
But at the traffic lights we'd wait a while
When we're home all I'd want to do is play

I love my mom, she does every thing for me
Oh my mom, my mom how lovely us she.

Sufyan Mussadiq Ahmed (12)
The Earls High School, Halesowen

Life Is A Cocoon Of Darkness

Life is a cocoon of darkness
Briefly illuminated by the most deceiving light
A never-ending struggle for fire
To reverse the mistakes once made

Deep in the abyss all is empty
Except for the momentous cries for help
Existence in this cold place is a bore
Concealed in the walls once free

The only escape is the final escape
The one that I would devote all hope
I reach my hands out, open arms
And fall into an endless sleep.

Jordan Crump (15)
The Earls High School, Halesowen

Theory Of Our Demon

Our demons
The things we keep locked in a chest
And we throw away the key
But they seem to break out and torture me
The hell burning eyes
I try and keep them in
But they seem to break through my barrier of smiles
The sudden anger in my eye
The anger in my voice
The words cutting through you like fire-lit knives
Or demons
The things we keep in a chest
And we try to throw away the key
But now mine are here to torture me!

Sophie Stibbs (16)
The Earls High School, Halesowen

My Nan

I love my nan for everything she'll do
She'll keep on fighting even with the flu
My nan's a warrior, fresh from the fight
My nan's a genius, clever and bright
My nan's quite happy, she's hardly ever down
My nan's a joker, a bit of a clown
She has got two children, one is my dad
She has turned him into a proper lad
My nan's a princess straight from her palace
My nan's got a granddaughter called Alice
My nan's a hero and a part of me
My nan loves her cheese, especially brie
Even though she's over sixty-seven
I would hate to see her leave for Heaven.

Max Williams (13)
The Earls High School, Halesowen

Why I Love You

I love you because you are there for me
And I love how you can smile all the time
Your wisdom and smiles have taught me to see
That your favourite colour isn't lime
You cook the food every day for us
And do the washing up all on your own
Even though all we do is make a fuss
You never, ever, ever raise your tone
The rays of sunshine that come from the sky
Makes me feel that you will look after me
And you are always telling me don't lie
And you say, 'Make a nice cup of tea'
I'll always love you from death and beyond
And that love eternal can't break our bond.

Laura King (12)
The Earls High School, Halesowen

My Mom

My mom, I know she is my one true mum and I care
I know I will cherish her dearly
For she is oh so very dearly rare
She is the one I love and care for really
She watches me grow and helps me through my ways
It is clear to see we will be a team
She lets me see the love for her for days
I know that she will always be in my dream
I love her lots as it is clear to see
I'll care for her and give her what she needs
I know for sure that we can clearly be
A team of one together as this reads
I'll love my mum forever and ever
Even when it changes the weather.

Chantelle Smith (13)
The Earls High School, Halesowen

Look!

Look!
Can't you see her?
She's standing right in front of you,
Can't you hear her?
She's calling out to you.

Heart thrashing,
Head pounding,
A constant drumbeat,
Beating, beating.

Look!
Can't you hear her?
No! Because she's dying,
Fading, this drumming is so suffocating.

Pounding, it's pounding,
A hole expanding,
I'm being compressed,
Contorted like a snake strangles its prey,

I'm immobilised,
Annihilation,
Why don't you help her?

Answer me!

Look! Look at her!
She's dead,
Skin burning,
Glass breaking.

Look!
Can't you see me?
I'm standing right in front of you,
And
I'm
Shouting.

Katie Lloyd
The Kingswinford School, Kingswinford

Environment

Look out the window
All barren and bare
The natural beauty
That once was there.

The little critters
Who hid in the wood
From the men who left
More than footprints in mud.

The trees were cut
The branches were slashed
With axes and hammers
All nests were smashed.

The ice, it melts
The sea levels rise
Mankind destroys
In hope of a prize.

Climate changes
Fires are started
Because of us
Animals are parted.

So just to tell
This little tale
Of this world
Destroyed by Man's betrayal.

Elizabeth Thompson (13)
The Kingswinford School, Kingswinford

To The Moon And Back

I want to see the stars one day,
But that's not where I'm heading.
I thought that's what they invented me for,
And now I'm really dreading.

I don't know where I'm set to soar,
I hope it's somewhere fantastic.
One day I wish to reach the sky,
I'm so enthusiastic.

I wait and wait,
For my flames to roar.
I don't think I can wait,
Anymore.

They whisper tales of unforeseen weather,
And tracking issues also.
They don't know when I can finally fly high,
I desperately just want to go.

Maybe they'll let me zoom off soon,
But nobody really knows.
I can't wait to blast-off to a new place,
Ending all of my woes.

I want to see the stars one day,
But that's not where I'm heading.
I thought that's what they invented me for,
And now I'm really dreading.

Natasha Smith
The Kingswinford School, Kingswinford

Defining Love

Love is a blossoming flower,
Evolved from a single seed.
The outbreak of red petals,
Like the distinct flush on my cheeks.

Love is a spark ignited,
The sudden surge of butterflies,
The beating of my dancing heart,
With you I know that love never dies.

Love is an eternal flame,
Once lit, it never ends.
You're forever my favourite place,
Knowing we're more than friends.

Our story is a fairy tale,
You be the pencil, I'll be the paper.
Without sunlight, a flower perishes,
But you can be the light and my saviour.
In our fairy tale, we can live like Jack and Sally,
Or Jack and Rose smiling happily.

Rachel Tang
The Kingswinford School, Kingswinford

Best Friends

I will always be there for you,
Until the very end.
Comforting you when you're down,
Being your best friend.

I will laugh when you laugh,
Smile when you smile,
And if you shed a single tear,
I promise I'll be here.

Emily Heaton (14)
The Kingswinford School, Kingswinford

Living Life As Me

What people can't see are lies behind the eyes
To some it's no surprise
Trying to stop the tears
And hide your greatest fears
It is hard being me
The pain you will never see.

I go through things you wouldn't believe
Wearing my heart upon my sleeve
Behind closed doors
There will be roars
If you want to know what it is like to be me
I am sure you wouldn't want to see.

Life can be a struggle
More than I can juggle
All you can see is a smile
It will be gone in a while
One day I will be free
To live my life as me.

Abigail Grace Bentley
The Kingswinford School, Kingswinford

The Unicorn

There was a unicorn who could fly.
He liked to go really high.
He heard a loud sound,
And fell to the ground.
So now he's about to die . . .
He landed in a park,
His vision went all dark.
His vision was blurred,
An ambulance could be heard,
At least he is safe now..

Archie John Browne (14)
The Kingswinford School, Kingswinford

The Man With Red Hair

People walking everywhere,
People walking without a care,
A person sitting on a chair,
He just has to stare.

People everywhere,
Stare without a care,
Have to stare,
For the man with red hair.

The man with red hair,
He didn't care,
He didn't stare,
But people still glared.

The man with red hair,
Lay dead in the street,
Shot down where he stood,
He didn't make a peep.

Louis Bissell (14)
The Kingswinford School, Kingswinford

Nothingness

Can you hear it? Of course not
This is the sound that you have forgot.
This is the sound of emptiness
The loneliness, silentness and nothingness
I guess you can't feel it either
Pure nothingness seeping in deeper
I always look at the cold, grey ceiling
Constantly seeing how much I'm unfeeling
Their humble emotions I want and miss
But this is the life of us Dissimilis.

Katie Moore (14)
The Kingswinford School, Kingswinford

Beauty Of The Forest

Song of a forest
Sang by the birds
Where you escape the world
No human to be heard.

Leaves turn to fire
A fire we can control
Yellow, orange, red
The bright colours of happiness.

The majestic scents
Of buttercups and roses
On a canvas the colours light up
The different shades of the buttercup.

Butterflies flutter across the sky
Their colours sparkle in the sunlight
The forest is where you escape the world
No human to be heard.

Amber Charlton
The Kingswinford School, Kingswinford

Shattered Soul

Shattered soul, tattered mind
The way back is what I hope to find
I got lost between today and tomorrow
But each day is filled with sorrow
The smile I show can last a few seconds
I hope one day I'll get some new directions
To take me somewhere better
I will write you all a letter
I need to defeat this hurt and pain
Please, tell me I am not insane.

Ellie Moore (15)
The Kingswinford School, Kingswinford

What Is Love?

What is love?
Love is a twirling, swirling roller coaster,
There are ups, downs, twists and turns.

What is love?
Love smells like perfume,
Strong, hypnotising and full of power.

What is love?
Love tastes like dark, dark chocolate,
Rich, expensive and addictive.

What is love?
Love is a red, red rose,
Elegant, beautiful and full of passion.

But, what is love?

Charlotte Fereday
The Kingswinford School, Kingswinford

Islamic Rising

Islamic rising, allies join together,
To free the hostages, bring peace forever.
Terrorist attacks, military force,
Soldiers fight to destroy their cause.

They have seized Northern, Western Iraq and Syria
And influenced their law of Sharia.
Religious and ethnic minorities they kill in their masses,
With tactics used to rival the Nazis.
The world watches with outrage and fear,
Will military intervention bring an end to this near.

Islamic rising, allies join together
To free the hostages, bring peace forever.
Terrorist attacks, military force,
Soldiers fight to destroy their cause.

Sadie Smith (14)
The Kingswinford School, Kingswinford

Ordinary People

The sun shines brightly on the urban city
As ordinary people go about their day.
The night draws in slowly
The stars shone brightly
Street lamps fire up
Lighting the way for the ordinary people
Going about their day.

The splish, splash of the rain crashing down
Onto the normal, ordinary people going about their day
Umbrellas appear across the city
Window wipers sway up and down
As dark clouds hover above the city
And over the ordinary people driving home
As they go about their day.

Lewis Jones (13)
The Kingswinford School, Kingswinford

Fear Of The Future

A thousand possibilities awaiting in the stars,
But you're held back by a thousand mental scars,
You're afraid of getting older,
Knowing the fire in your hearts burning colder,
How can you work your entire life,
Knowing it could all end by the blade of a knife,
And what if you stayed conscious after death?
Knowing you're never again to take another breath,
Facing so many tears,
Brought on by too many fears,
Although you hold onto the moments of happiness,
Because without them our lives are worthless,
So be brave, be strong,
Think it won't get better? You're wrong.

Esther Plant
The Kingswinford School, Kingswinford

The End?

Her dad left her when she was a baby
Her mum treats her like she doesn't deserve to live
At school she's getting bullied
All her friends that she thought she had disappeared
Her mind is convincing her she's worthless
She's deceived by her own negative thoughts
Is this the end? she asks herself
Do I have a place to go . . .
As she holds the bottle of pills in her hand
Glancing at herself in the mirror
Already with sharp strikes of cuts up her arm
She takes the last dose of pills
Her last breath
Maybe it is the end.

Sharon Chitapa (14)
The Kingswinford School, Kingswinford

Current Affairs

Current affairs
Bring up the hairs
On the back of your neck
Maybe I should ask him to check.
Discussing about terrorists
Known as ISIS
They behead people and go to war
They record it on YouTube
And David Cameron's asked to send troops
To go knocking on their door
Talking about immigrants
Most of them are poor
A group called UKIP
Don't want them in the country anymore.

Suhayb Anjum (13)
The Kingswinford School, Kingswinford

◯ No Emotion

Flappy, excited, impatient, adrenaline rushing through my veins, bones, skin,
flying with the rest of me.
Sad, depressed, hurt, pain rushing through my veins, bones, skin,
sinking with the rest of me.
Anger, frustrated, mad, hate rushing through my veins, bones, skin,
breaking with the rest of me.
Patience, understanding, calm, relaxation rushing through my veins, bones,
skin,
resting with the rest of me.
Compassion, numb, dazed, fear rushing through my veins, bones, skin,
floating with the rest of me.
Keep your thoughts separate from your actions
and your mind separate from your brain and your heart?
That depends what controls you?

Payton Clifford
The Kingswinford School, Kingswinford

✊ Death

Death is a disease,
It comes for us all,
It happens to the best,
They always fall,
It puts us to the test.

Death is an enemy,
Keeps us at bay,
When people die they become a memory,
Death never goes away.

Death is a phantom,
Scurrying through the night,
Like a gunshot fired out of a Magnum,
It's no good trying to resist, you won't win the fight.

Brandon Bate (13)
The Kingswinford School, Kingswinford

For Alice

I see you struggle all the time,
But never do you complain.
It's clear you need a friend to help,
And to get you through this pain.

I might not be able to help you,
I can't fully understand.
But I'll always care about you,
I'll try to lend a helping hand.

Every day seems to get worse, I know
You find it hard to cope.
So I'll be a shoulder to cry on,
A friend to give you hope.

Niamh Stapley (13)
The Kingswinford School, Kingswinford

The Souls Of War

Soldiers receiving pain
Lost in the blood rain
With nothing to gain
But breaths before death

War torn bodies stiff as rocks
Lying tied up in blood like a clock
With no key to undo the lock
Stuck left to drown helplessly

Syria's soulless soldiers lying dead
Wishing they could rest in their cosy beds
Bullets shot through men's heads
What has this world come to?

Tara Davies (14)
The Kingswinford School, Kingswinford

Waiting For A Better You

It's like everyone's waiting for a different me,
I never know how to make them see,
I don't know how to act and I don't know how to be,
I should know it's always you and never we.

I'm unsure why I stay,
Every single day.
I wish there was a way,
To forget what you say.

I don't like you,
I bet you hate me too.
Everything I do,
Is ruined by you.

Louise V Finch (14)
The Kingswinford School, Kingswinford

Music's Dead

Catchy beat with meaningless words.
No emotion and no heart.
Repetitive and offensive,
From finish to start,
Pointless songs; no longer art.

Singers can't sing,
Playing no instruments.
Just all enticements,
In it for the money,
No originality.
Someone killed music,
And took away its heart and soul.

Katie Brigstock (14)
The Kingswinford School, Kingswinford

Grammy Awards

Striving for the best all year round,
Flashing lights and beating sound.
Never giving up, determined to be the best,
Doing what they do, not worried about the rest.
Portraying their talents in the very best way,
Making a living each and every day.
The Grammy Awards are their final reward,
The winners voted by the public's accord.

Ebony Salmon (14)
The Kingswinford School, Kingswinford

Anger

Anger is a stormy ocean
Anger is a fireball glowing
Anger is a gust of wind
Anger is a volcano about to erupt
Anger is a tornado
Anger is a devil with dark red eyes
Anger is a fire waiting to happen.

Harry Dimmock (13)
The Kingswinford School, Kingswinford

Trial (I Plead Not Guilty)

Here I stand, waiting for my verdict
Waiting to be sentenced
Waiting to be labelled

Around me, I am surrounded
By my familiars
By the jury

Their stares pierce my mind
They scrutinise me
They take into account my face, my clothes, my hair
They silently and ruthlessly take apart everything I am

Suddenly, every detail of my life is revealed
My deepest and darkest secrets become evidence
I hear them whispering accusations of guilt
Their thoughts screaming, '*criminal!*'

My innocence is taken away, stripped from me
I am tainted, branded a sinner
By the very ones who had forced me to sin

The doors open

Abruptly, their murmurs quieten
They are reduced to a petrified silence
They rise
The judges have arrived

We wait

Immediately, we are rendered nameless, faceless

We are nothing to them
But merely numbers and statistics
We are ticks and crosses
We are failures and achievements

The verdict is rendered null and void
Because no matter how innocent we are
We are all punished
We are all sentenced
To 18 years.

Emily Choudhury (17)
The Sixth Form College Solihull, Solihull

Trust

An arm stretched around hunched shoulders.
My arm.
Your shoulders.
A hand placed gently on a trembling, icy hand.
Linked little fingers; 'I'll protect you.
I promise.'

Do I put my trust into something I know I shouldn't?
It's a backwards fall into your outstretched arms
Because I'm never quite sure if you're going to
Catch me.

Reciprocation is too complex for me to comprehend.
The darkness that surrounds another person's thoughts is suffocating.
You fuel my downfall.
You make me worse.

You collapse.
I break your fall.
You can trust me.

I promise I'll protect you.
I tie my little finger
With yours.
I feel the chill
As I rest my warm hand
On yours
To comfort
You.
You lean
Up against me
And I place my arm
Around your curling back.

I did not know the poison
On your tongue until it was too far into my bloodstream,
Like chemicals infecting my body.

Ashton Collard (17)
The Sixth Form College Solihull, Solihull

Dubiety

Young age and all these decisions,
Set rules and all these provisions.

If we are to know now, is there a pressure to know later?
Could it be possible I made you a wager?

Free the young mind and let the creative juices flow:
Dismissing creativity can feel like a major blow.

Intellectuality is key, that's for sure
I envy their wisdom, cleverness and mind's decor.

Education for the masses includes memory, not knowledge
Kids can feel stuck in places like college.

Let us learn what we want to do
That's the goal, isn't it true?

We're supposed to grow up, to be filled with passion,
Not sitting at a desk waiting for the magic to happen.

Decisions are hard, that is what I've concluded,
Having no future plans with society's high expectations can make us feel quite
alluded.

I hate the pressure that is bore down on us young adults,
We will only succeed if we get the 'right' results.

Is it wrong to say that we need more time?
Or am I wrong because we're supposedly in our 'prime'?

So I guess I'll leave now and say one last thing
What knowledge can future planning bring?

We work, work, work for that one big chance
But will we ever finish this everlasting dance?

Leela Doherty
The Sixth Form College Solihull, Solihull

LGBT Prejudice

You see the rainbow, you see the love,
yet you shield your eyes.
You can't accept, you can't embrace,
your narrow-mindedness is aged, moulded,
on false ideas.

Why? Because it disagrees?
Break the mould, it's not hard!
It doesn't affect you but you take it so personally,
you hurt, you chant, you protest
and suffering is your reward,
and you feed on it like ravenous animals.

Change is good, you shy away,
pride is strong and your placards are weak,
we don't hurt you but
offence-taken,
you bury your head in the sand
and I hope you choke on the grit, the concepts with no art.

Our colours burn bright,
we will stay strong, prepare for a fight,
you need to adapt
to the new world,
stop relying on religion, or morals
and get over yourself, open your arms.

We may forgive,
but forgiveness is not offered to those with bloody hands and tainted mouths.

Georgia Lees-Lowe
The Sixth Form College Solihull, Solihull

Empty Heart

True, my love will come and go,
But my empty heart remains
The long and cold embraces
From the man I'll never name

His heart is cold and feelings gone
But my hands are warm in his
The barren world around me
Where he is all there is

They stare and point as we walk by
And I see them fear for me
But being with him is all I am
And all I'm meant to be

This night may be my last alone
Tomorrow is my fate
A gown of white and roses red
Until the altar where he waits

The days of sun are over
And I understand their fear
The marks his words had made
Have suddenly appeared

True, my love will come and go
But my heart and bruises stay
The fierce and violent slashes
From my lover's caring ways.

Phoebe Cooper (16)
The Sixth Form College Solihull, Solihull

The Epic Of The Vegetables

Eggplant, eggplant
Purple and green
Eggplant, eggplant
Aids your spleen
Eggplant, eggplant
Au-ber-gine

Mushroom, mushroom
Good to fry
Mushroom, mushroom
Makes me cry
Mushroom, mushroom
Fun fun-gi

Cabbage, cabbage
Leafy and white
Cabbage, cabbage
Eat day or night
Cabbage, cabbage
Veg-e-mite

Radish, radish
Pungent or sweet
Radish, radish
Eat with meat
Radish, radish
Root el-ite.

Priyesh Sthankiya (17)
The Sixth Form College Solihull, Solihull

The Storm

It all starts with a cloud; the sky starts changing,
She falls to the floor, her energy draining.
The wind comes too strong, you can see her fading.

But in the eye of the storm, the light fights on.

He fears it's too late as the rain starts pouring,
And the wind screams the words 'lonely' and 'boring',
As the chorus of the false thoughts starts roaring.

The light sings his song of comfort and warmth.

As the wind slowly dies, the song can be heard,
She realises those thoughts are quite absurd,
But still, her view on reality is blurred.

The clouds break, and the light is seen.

He knows he's safe now, but approaches with care,
The storm is silent, but rain falls from the stare
Of unblinking eyes, with too much to bare.

The light gives its final push to break through.

As the tears disappear in the light's strong heat
The eyes of the two, inseparable, meet.
The cloud never goes, but for now it is weak.

The smiles show the light is worth more than the storm.

Kim Brilus
The Sixth Form College Solihull, Solihull

The Change

Loud
Tonnes of bombs going off all at once,
I'm drowning in irritation.
Frustration, anger
Or is it confusion?

White
Not like innocence, it's just bright,
So white, it's nothing.
Empty, hollow
Or is it just clear?

Cold
There is a lack of heat, it is noticeable,
Though not yet missed.
Bitter, raw
Or is it just gone?

Forward
Towards the future, the past is now over,
The absence of childhood.
Lonely, afraid
Or is this just growing up?

Kashala Whittingham (16)
The Sixth Form College Solihull, Solihull

The War We Were Never Meant To See

Through black and white streets,
No colour blossoms,
Except the crimson stream,
We were never meant to see.

Through censored fields,
A mother's muted weeping
Fills the distant air with sadness,
We were never meant to feel.

In far-off lands of sand
And soulless soldiers marching
To a tuneless beat,
We were never meant to hear.

But the war still rages,
For the fearful
And the valiant still in never-ending conflict,
That we shall never need to see.

James Warden
The Sixth Form College Solihull, Solihull

When I Think Of Aurora

Oh, when I think of Aurora,
So radiant and so serene,
Fingers dusted a rosy hue
I groan with eyelids tightly shut.
She drags me from my blissful warmth,
Her golden chariot gleaming.
I cannot deny her rousing,
When rosy fingered dawn appears.

Amy Wilson
The Sixth Form College Solihull, Solihull

Blank

Poems are really hard to write,
Picking the subject takes all night,
Pointless searching makes you aware,
No ideas can be found there.
Your brain, that is.

You sit for hours, days, months and years
And worse than all your deepest fears,
Nothing comes to mind at all,
Under pressure brains can stall.
Annoying, that is.

Then after a painful long wait,
You know it's really just too late,
You choose to just write away,
See what happens come what may.
Dangerous, that is.

Hannah Biddle
The Sixth Form College Solihull, Solihull

Aphrodite

Snip, snip, snip
It flies through the air
Splosh, splosh, splosh
It lands in the sea
Froth, froth, froth
Out comes a clam
Creak, creak, creak
Inside is a pearl
Gasp, gasp, gasp
The pearl is a girl
Pretty, pretty, pretty
It's Aphrodite!

Amna Raja (17)
The Sixth Form College Solihull, Solihull

Lucifer

You only see the mask I hide behind.
Down here, the dark is suffocating me.
The hated villain with the hero's mind
Who dwells behind the locks holding the key.
However strong I seem, I know I'm weak;
Keeping the truth so you have one to blame.
I must remain alone, remain the freak,
Remain the hated target in your game.
I wouldn't bow to humans down on Earth
So Father sent me down to Hell to stay.
I know I'm more than what you think I'm worth
But reputations don't just fade away.
I'm meant to live in Heaven not in Hell
But life is cruel to you when you rebel.

Mei-Ling Rhodes
The Sixth Form College Solihull, Solihull

Web Of Sins

You told me to be honest
I opened my mouth and you bared your teeth
Your words like acid inside my head.
You told me to be myself
I lifted my layers and your claws ran deep
Metal through my veins.
You told me to earn your affection
I realised you had none.
My head, my skin, it will never be the same now.
Hated is a kiss compared to how I feel.
What have you done?
What have I done?
It's done.
Remember old sins increase eroding of your soul.

Abigail Davies (17)
The Sixth Form College Solihull, Solihull

YOUNG WRITERS INFORMATION

We hope you have enjoyed reading this book – and that you will continue to in the coming years.

If you're a young writer who enjoys reading and creative writing, or the parent of an enthusiastic poet or story writer, do visit our website **www.youngwriters.co.uk**. Here you will find free competitions, workshops and games, as well as recommended reads, a poetry glossary and our blog.

If you would like to order further copies of this book, or any of our other titles, give us a call or visit **www.youngwriters.co.uk**.

Young Writers,
Remus House
Coltsfoot Drive,
Peterborough,
PE2 9BF

(01733) 890066 / 898110
info@youngwriters.co.uk